The Psychic Vegan Cookbook

The Psychic Vegan Cookbook

Henrietta Flores

photographs by
Cory Mac a'Ghobhainn

Published by Dagmar Miura
Los Angeles
www.dagmarmiura.com

The Psychic Vegan Cookbook

Copyright © 2018 Dagmar Miura
All rights reserved. No part of this book may be used or reproduced in any manner whatsoever without prior written permission except in the case of brief quotations embodied in critical articles or reviews. For information, address Dagmar Miura, dagmarmiura@gmail.com, or visit our website at www.dagmarmiura.com.

This book is intended to provide helpful and accurate information. The publisher and author disclaim any liability, loss, damage, or injury caused by the use or application of the contents of this work. No warranty, express or implied, is delivered by the author or publisher with respect to the contents of this work.

Photographed with a Google Pixel 2.

First published 2018

ISBN: 978-1-942267-49-2

Contents

Introduction — 1
About the Mason Braithwaite Series — 1

About Veganism — 3
Animal Welfare — 3
Environmental Impact — 4
Nutrition — 4
Books and Resources — 10

Nonstandard Ingredients and Tools — 11
Soy Products — 11
Seitan — 13
Deli Slices and Cheese Shreds — 13
Nutritional Yeast — 13
Tamari — 14
Tahini — 14
High-Speed Blender — 14
Raw Nuts — 15

Breakfast — 19
Espresso — 20
Oatmeal — 22
French Toast — 23
Pancakes — 24
Muesli — 26
Fruit Smoothie — 27
Tofu Scramble — 29

Starters — 31
Guacamole — 32
Quesadillas — 33
Hummus — 34
Veggie Pâté — 36
Tabbouleh — 37

Soups — 39
- Raw Tomato and Red Pepper Soup — 40
- Gazpacho — 42
- Parsnip Pearl Barley Soup — 43

Salads — 45
- Spicy Cucumber Salad — 47
- Tofu Caprese Salad — 48
- Croutons — 49
- Caesar Salad — 50
- Rationalist Dressing — 52
- Sweet Mustard Dressing — 53
- Asian Ginger Dressing — 54

Mains — 57
- Pesto on Zucchini Noodles — 58
- Teriyaki Tofu — 59
- Socca — 60
- Thin-Crust Pizza with Sliced Red Peppers — 62
- Baked Eggplant — 64
- Mac and Cheese — 67
- White Bean Chili — 68
- Curry — 69
- Onion, Pepper, and Mushroom Hash — 70
- Cold Soba Noodles with Dipping Sauce — 72
- Roasted Squash — 73
- Cold Chinese Noodles with Sesame Sauce — 75
- Vegan Ricotta and Spinach-Stuffed Shells — 76
- Seitan Stroganoff — 77
- Fried Tempeh with Plum Sauce — 78
- Seitan Wellington and Mushroom Gravy — 80
- Tempeh Salad — 83

Sides — 85

- Roasted Green Cauliflower Steaks — 86
- Crusty Bread — 88
- 1950s Peas and Carrots — 89
- Mushroom Gravy — 90
- Atomic Pinto Beans — 92

Desserts — 95

- Meringue Cookies — 96
- Baked Doughnuts — 97
- Peanut Butter Cookies — 98
- Oatmeal Cookies — 100
- Secret Avocado Chocolate Mousse — 101
- Red Velvet Cake — 102
- Zucchini Bread — 105
- Chocolate Layer Cake — 106
- Pineapple Upside-Down Cake — 108
- Apple Pie — 110

Kitchen Staples — 113

- Salsa Fresca — 114
- Chimichurri — 116
- Tomato Sauce — 117
- Spicy Slather Sauce — 118
- Cashew Cheese Sauce — 119
- Nacho Cheese Sauce — 120
- Aioli — 121

Acknowledgments — 123

About the Author — 125

About the Photographer — 125

Index — 127

Introduction

First up, I'm not psychic. The title of the book relates to the protagonist of the Mason Braithwaite Paranormal Mystery Series. He's a charming ethical vegan who makes his living as a psychic investigator. Because he's not much of a cook, and also because he's actually a fictional character, I took on the task of relating recipes for some of the food described in the book series, along with other everyday staples for contemporary cooks, including a couple of my personal favorites.

None of the dishes in this book are especially intricate, and most of the ingredients are easy to obtain. Some of the more esoteric items might not be available in a local grocery store but can easily be obtained online.

I hope you get some inspiration in these pages for your personal vegan journey!

About the Mason Braithwaite Paranormal Mystery Series

Vegan food is a big part of the Mason series, to the point that some readers said, "I wish there was a cookbook." Psychic investigator Mason has a great living arrangement, with his boyfriend, Ned, an ethical vegan who's passionate about vegan cooking, and their roommate, the folk singer Peggy Pregnant, a renaissance woman with mad kitchen chops.

No one is ever quite sure whether Mason gets results with actual psychic power or his more mundane flatfooting, but fueled by caffeine and great vegan cuisine, navigating the rarified heights and gritty depths of Los Angeles on his trusty bicycle, the disheveled redhead manages to resolve some intractable mysteries. The body count stays comfortably at zero in Mason's work as he pursues crooked CEOs, grifters, and identity thieves, hunts for treasure, and tangles with strippers, aliens, Freemasons, and paranormal entities. His tools are his psychic intuition, time travel, and the odd séance, and when things go awry Ned and Peggy are usually around to help pick up the pieces.

Read more about the series at **mason.dagmarmiura.com**.

About Veganism

Animal Welfare

If you're already committed to eating vegan, skip ahead, there's nothing new for you here. If you're thinking about it but aren't quite there, the best reason to go vegan is simple: making the choice not to eat animal products reduces the suffering of sentient creatures. You can find a stunning amount of information online about animal welfare, and the science is clear: the more we learn about animals—that they use reasoning, hold grudges, have friendships—the fewer differences we find between our species and others. It doesn't only apply to primates, or even to mammals: octopuses have repeatedly been observed using tools and even pranking their prey, and dozens of species of birds use reasoning as well as tools. Our understanding of our fellow creatures is evolving. One hundred and fifty years ago, Charles Darwin shocked the world by suggesting we were even related to other animals rather than being specially placed on this planet by a supernatural entity. When tool use was discovered among chimpanzees in the last century, at first many biologists refused to believe it.

My vision of an ideal future is that using animals as part of our food supply will become a shameful historical curiosity, like killing people in religious ceremonies, conducting medical experiments on prison inmates, or enslaving other people. That won't happen in my lifetime, but going vegan is definitely a commitment to being on the right side of history. Any vegan can tell you that nothing feels as liberating or as reaffirming as knowing that you've helped reduce suffering in the world.

A final note on this topic: food marketers would have us believe that animal products can somehow be cruelty-free. This is often implied by terms like "free-range," "cage-free," "hormone-free," and "natural."

It's a bald-faced lie: there is no way to produce meat, dairy, and eggs that isn't torture for the animal.

Environmental Impact

Simply put, our society's level of consumption is not sustainable. Most people are aware of this, but the mainstream frames it in terms of our use of fossil fuels. Not as many are aware of the destructive impact of eating animals and animal products. The UN Food and Agriculture Organization says that 18 percent of greenhouse gas emissions come from animal agriculture—that's more than all the driving, shipping, trucking, and airplane travel we do, which accounts for 13 percent.

Half the water we use in California goes to producing meat and dairy products, so it always made me scratch my head during the drought when people would do things like shower with a bucket to collect water for their houseplants or let their lawns die, but then go chow down on a cheeseburger or frozen yogurt. One thousand gallons of water are required to produce a gallon of cow's milk; 477 gallons of water are used to produce a pound of eggs—the list goes on. Going vegan will instantly and dramatically reduce your carbon footprint and your consumption of other resources, and far more effectively than switching to LED bulbs or buying that electric car. Cowspiracy (**www.cowspiracy.com/facts**) has an extensive list of these statistics and the scientific studies that reveal them.

Nutrition

The healthiest way to eat is incredibly simple: vegan food, not including processed foods. The 2011 film *Forks Over Knives* explains the health benefits of eating this way in great detail, but the concept can be expressed in a simple phrase: eat plant-based whole foods.

That said, this book is about everyday vegan cooking, not avoiding processed foods, but almost all the ingredients used in the recipes are simple and minimally processed. When a recipe calls for cocoa powder, it means a brand with an ingredient list of one item, cacao. When applesauce is used, it means one ingredient, apples. The same goes for peanut butter; it's easy to find brands that have a lot of added sugar and a long list of chemicals. Think simple: the fewer ingredients, the better. The reason many people choose tamari instead of soy sauce is similar; soy sauce has a long list of ingredients, while tamari has three or four, all recognizable. It's galling that food products with few or no additives cost so much more than sugar- and chemical-laden products, but keep in mind that it makes little sense to cheap out on your health.

The Protein Myth

The human body doesn't need animal protein. If healthy vegan firefighters and Olympic weightlifters aren't evidence enough, there's hard science. Of the twenty amino acids that our bodies need to synthesize proteins, eleven can be synthesized by the body, and nine need to be consumed in food. A diet with a variety of grains, legumes, and vegetables provides all of them. Diets too high in protein have been linked to heart disease, impaired kidney function, and osteoporosis. Find links to the scientific research and published results in "The Protein Myth" by the Physicians Committee for Responsible Medicine, **https://goo.gl/gG6959**.

The Dairy Myth

Milk is for babies, and most people in the world sensibly don't consume it past childhood. Anecdotally, osteoporosis is far less common in places like East Asia, where people consume far less dairy than Americans do. Far from being good for you, milk has been shown in scientific research to contribute

to osteoporosis. Dairy products acidify the body, and to compensate, your body pulls calcium out of your bones to neutralize the acidity. The net result is that if you consume dairy products, you lose more calcium than you consume. Vivian Goldschmidt spells it out and cites the research papers in "Debunking the Milk Myth," https://goo.gl/yw3KqM.

Hydrogenated Oils

In the past decade, trans fats have essentially been banned from the U.S. food industry. This is a positive step that will improve human health, as overwhelming evidence links trans fats to heart disease. In the hundred years before that, margarine was a popular vegan substitute for butter. Most margarine was made with hydrogenated oil: vegetable oil treated with hydrogen, which gave it the desirable quality of remaining solid at room temperature. The problem with hydrogenation is that it creates trans fats. We don't see products labeled "margarine" anymore because that name implies that it contains unhealthy trans fats. Many types of healthier nonhydrogenated oils have been developed into vegan spreads that stay solid at room temperature. K. D. Angle-Traegner runs down the various brands available (https://goo.gl/GurT18), with the added bonus of discussing palm oil, whether we should be eating it or not, and which brands contain it.

Food Fads

In the 1980s there was a food fad that saw a wide range of processed food marketed as "low fat" and "fat free." The marketing wisdom was that eating fat made you fat, so avoiding fat completely would make you thin. Although the fad still lingers at the supermarket, the current thinking is that easily accessible carbohydrates like sugar and pasta and bread are a bigger problem in weight gain. A decade from now, the dieting trend will likely involve some new prohibition or food fad. The best food advice is the simplest: eat a varied diet of plant-based whole foods, and as any honest doctor will tell you, lose weight by eating less and exercising more. Some of the wackier food fads and their claims:

Superfoods

Maca powder, goji berries, chia seeds, açaí—every few months the miraculous health properties and jaw-dropping levels of nutrients of a relatively unknown food product are suddenly revealed. The term *superfood* has no legal meaning and no regulation on its use, so a food factory can plaster the word on anything, which means it has no meaning. Think of the way *natural* is used to sell things like heavily processed desserts, potato chips, and dissected chickens. No single food has magical nutritional properties, and eating a varied diet of legumes, grains, and vegetables is the best way to get full nutrition. Just as vitamin supplements are falling out of favor these days as people get wise to their spurious utility, consumers should be skeptical of the vague nutrition and health claims made for superfoods.

Making specific medical claims is another matter entirely, and the Food and Drug Administration routinely reprimands marketers claiming that superfoods cure specific diseases, as in 2006 when goji berries were sold as curing high blood pressure, gum disease, and even cancer. When the next food fad comes along from the Himalayas or the Amazon, keep in mind that "superfood" is a marketing term and has nothing to do with nutrition or science. That kind of marketing can even damage the communities where these products originate, as in the Andes when the price of quinoa skyrocketed because of marketing-driven demand in wealthy nations. Local people couldn't afford to buy it anymore, even though it had been a staple food for centuries. Among many others, Tom Philpott lays it out in *Mother Jones* (**https://goo.gl/ntFErS**).

Wheat Gluten

If wheat was expensive and available only to high-end consumers in specialty supermarkets, it would

be called a superfood. It's extremely nutritious and healthy when it's not bleached and stripped of its fiber. The only people who need to avoid wheat are those with celiac disease, a legitimate documented condition akin to an allergy to gluten. Ask any diagnosed celiac what it's like to eat wheat, and they'll tell you it's not a matter of feeling a little tired or bloated; eating wheat makes them seriously ill. If you think you might be celiac, see a doctor. If you think you're eating too much wheat, seek more variety in your diet rather than turning to processed gluten-free foods, often loaded with sugar to compensate for the taste of less nutritious grains. I recently saw a jug of laundry detergent labeled "gluten-free." That's a marketing-generated fad if I've ever seen one.

Sugar

An article in the *Journal of the American Medical Association* in 2017 claimed that the sugar industry secretly funded research fifty years ago to refute the connection between sugar and heart disease and point the blame at fat instead. It worked, and sugar has only recently come under fire for its deleterious effects on human health. The issue seems to be that sugar raises triglycerides levels in the body. There is evidence, however, that a vegan diet reduces triglycerides. Until there is more evidence, perhaps the solution is moderation. People have been consuming refined sugar for centuries, although not in the quantities we get in junk foods.

The Paleo Diet

If you were to truly eat like a Stone Age human, you'd be eating a whole lot of unrefined plant foods, bugs, and the occasional mouse or squirrel, bones and all. A diet that claims to be Paleolithic but includes things like bacon, coconut butter, and almond flour smells like a marketed food trend, and indeed some segments of the medical community, so enthusiastic just a few years ago about the healing power of eating all that animal protein, have backed off recommending the diet. Some vegan activists theorize that paleo is just an excuse for those wanting to assuage their guilt to eat as much animal flesh as they want and claim it as a necessary evil for their unique constitution. *Scientific American* runs down the science in "Why the Paleo Diet Is Half-Baked" (https://goo.gl/ER4wwN).

Books and Resources

Forks Over Knives, www.forksoverknives.com. Recipes and uplifting ideas stemming from the 2011 documentary film outlining the scientific evidence that degenerative diseases can be stopped or reversed with a whole-food plant-based diet.

Alicia C. Simpson, *Quick and Easy Vegan Comfort Food* (The Experiment, 2009). Atlanta-based Simpson is a culinary genius, creating delicious versions of familiar dishes.

Celine Steen and Joni Marie Newman, *500 Vegan Recipes* (Fair Winds, 2009). All the basics and hundreds more.

Karina Inkster, *Vegan Vitality* (Helios, 2014). A specialist in health and aging, Inkster provides a roadmap for living a healthy, active, plant-based life.

Nonstandard Ingredients and Tools

Soy Products

Despite the fact that soy is extremely nutritious and a great vegetable source of protein, in the last decade or so there has been a tendency in some circles to demonize soy products as carcinogenic, or that soy messes up the body's estrogen levels. Vegan activists have traced the source of some of this information to big-money industry organizations whose interests lie in maintaining the meat-eating status quo. Like most things, the science seems to imply that moderation will obviate any of the purported danger. People who are getting too much soy, paradoxically, are the ones exclusively eating junk food and processed food, as soy is an ubiquitous ingredient in that stuff. A plant-based, whole-food diet with soy as a chosen ingredient contains a lot less soy than a junk-food diet. If soy is still just too terrifying, there are many other ways to get protein in a vegan diet.

Tofu

If you don't already know and love tofu, the thing to remember is that it's an ingredient that takes on the flavors of what it's prepared with. It's an acquired taste on its own, but just as you wouldn't eat bread flour on its own, tofu should be cooked in sauces or with vegetables. It also makes amazing puddings in a high-speed blender, and adds richness to soups.

Tempeh

Originally from Indonesia, tempeh gets its grainy texture from whole soybeans, fermented until they form

a solid mass. Because it's closer to a whole food, it has even more protein and better nutrition than tofu. Sliced thinly and doused with tamari, it fries up like bacon. Crumbled in tomato sauce, it adds density. Doused with teriyaki sauce on the grill, it's a perfect accompaniment to grilled veggies.

Seitan

Made from wheat flour by removing the starch component, leaving the glutinous protein, seitan makes a satisfying meaty source of protein. Because it's mostly gluten, it's unsuitable for anyone with celiac disease or those who've bought into the nebulous gluten-free trend. It's possible to make your own seitan from wheat flour, or save the labor and buy dried seitan, which is called vital wheat gluten. It holds up nicely in sauces, and can be sliced for sandwiches or slathered with gravy (page 90) to accompany vegetables.

Soy Crumbles, Deli Slices, and Cheese Shreds

There are some delicious processed food products available that mimic meat and dairy. Apart from Earth Balance and vegan mayo, these products aren't used in the recipes in this book, as the focus is on simpler ingredients. But if you're down with processed foods, go for it—there's hamburger replacer, faux turkey slices, even cheddar and mozzarella.

Nutritional Yeast

Many vegan cooks consider these dried yellow flakes an essential ingredient. Nutritional yeast adds a cheesy flavor to savory dishes, and when used in smaller quantities it adds a delicious umami component. Yeast is grown in a sweet medium and then "deactivated," meaning the yeast cells are killed, unlike the live yeast used in baking and brewing. Nutritional yeast is sometimes fortified with vitamin B_{12}, which isn't common in the vegan diet, and it contains lots of other nutrition and even a few calories.

Many recipes in this book use nutritional yeast, and like any fundamental ingredient, it has myriad other uses—sprinkle it on popcorn with some salt and lime zest; the flavor will blow your mind. It's unusual to see nutritional yeast at a mainstream supermarket, but if you don't live near an alternative or health-food market, it's easy to obtain on the Internet.

Tamari

Tamari can be swapped for soy sauce for any use, and doing so is a good idea. The taste difference is indistinguishable, but tamari has just three simple ingredients, while soy sauce usually includes a long list of unpronounceable chemicals. I made the switch in 2009 when CNN reported that manufacturers in China were using human hair, collected from barbershops and salons, as an ingredient in soy sauce. One of the most common tamari brands, San-J, brews its tamari in the United States and Japan; both countries have a good record on food contamination and counterfeiting.

Tahini

Tahini is really just a nut butter—pulverized sesame seeds. It's used in a couple of recipes in this book to add depth and flavor. If you can't find a jar of it at the market, you can make it in a high-speed blender; just blend sesame seeds at high speed for a couple of minutes.

High-Speed Blender

Often portrayed in the mainstream media as a decadent or pretentious kitchen tool, in vegan cooking a high-speed or high-performance blender is all

but essential. It's not necessary to buy a top-of-the-line model—Vitamix, for example, sells refurbished blenders that can be nearly half the price of their own high-end models.

Raw Nuts

It has always amazed me that nuts aren't more central to the way we eat. They're a whole food packed with nutrition and healthy oils. Almonds add texture and flavor in several recipes in this book, and in things like pesto (page 58) and as a salad topping, it's possible to switch out almonds for pecans or walnuts, or vice versa. Cashews are so versatile and ubiquitous in vegan cooking that they get their own section:

Cashews

Cashews can do a lot, adding creaminess and body to sauces without adding a strong flavor. Raw cashews are best for vegan cooking, rather than roasted, and don't buy them salted. If you don't use them very quickly, they keep nicely in the freezer. Buy cashew pieces, as they tend to be much cheaper than whole cashews—you're going to be pulverizing them anyway.

The Recipes

Breakfast

Espresso

Mason Braithwaite drinks a lot of coffee, claiming that it brings him up to the same speed everyone else is already at. In one of the novels he explains to a mentee that he drinks espresso because you get the caffeine kick without all the water. You might think it's too bitter to stomach, but anything worthwhile takes time to get into. Another mistaken belief about this liquid gold is that it has a high caffeine content; in fact, a shot of espresso has less caffeine than a cup of your World War II–style drip coffee that's been sitting in a carafe at the diner all morning.

In Europe and in some coffeehouses in this country, you can get a "short" or a "long" shot of espresso, differentiated only by the amount of water that is forced through the ground beans. Mason likes it short, because if you go long, he says, why not just drink cowboy coffee—or tea? Some automatic home espresso machines let you run the shot long or short, and some have a fixed setting. With a stove-top pot, the kind shown at right, you can control the amount of water expressed by taking it off the heat.

The big chain coffeehouses won't know what you're talking about if you ask for it short or long, but don't be put off if you don't like the flavor of what they're serving; every chain or indie coffeehouse roasts its beans differently, so try another shop. The best thing about ordering espresso in a coffeehouse is that it's much cheaper, faster, and lower in calories than any sweetened milky drink.

When he makes it for other people, Mason serves the espresso shot with a slice of lemon rind. It's a matter of taste as to whether that improves the flavor of the coffee or not, but if you want to try it, the best technique is just to squeeze the rind to spritz it into the cup, rather than dropping it in or wiping it on the rim.

Oatmeal

It may seem like oatmeal isn't something you'd need a recipe for, but I've perfected my own techniques, which I present here. Raw oats come in several forms, differentiated by how quickly they cook, which corresponds to how quickly your body absorbs the carbs. Don't bother with the quick or instant oats, because old-fashioned oats cook almost as quickly and will stay with you longer. Irish or steel-cut oats take forever to cook but are arguably healthier because they take longer to digest.

WITH OLD-FASHIONED OATS

1 cup old-fashioned oats

1½ cups water

¼ teaspoon salt

WITH STEEL-CUT OATS

2¼ cups water

¾ cup steel-cut oats

¼ teaspoon salt

WITH OLD-FASHIONED OATS

Put the oats and the salt in a saucepan and cover with the water. Bring to a boil.

Reduce the heat to medium. Stirring constantly, cook until the oatmeal reaches a pleasant consistency, about 2 minutes.

WITH STEEL-CUT OATS

In a saucepan, bring the water to a boil. Add the oats and the salt, and reduce to a simmer.

Cook for 15 minutes, up to 20 minutes if you want creamier, less chewy oatmeal.

GARNISHES

Mandatory for oatmeal in Ned's kitchen are brown sugar and soy milk or nut milk. Earth Balance or another vegan butter does it for some people, and don't forget blueberries or apple slices.

French Toast

Less work than you might think, and less fussy than pancakes, french toast demands to be served with maple syrup and berries. Cutting the slices of bread in half before soaking makes them easier to cook.

- 1 ripe banana
- 1 tablespoon cornstarch
- ¾ cup soy milk or nut milk
- ¼ teaspoon salt
- ¼ teaspoon cinnamon
- ⅛ teaspoon nutmeg
- ½ teaspoon nutritional yeast (optional)
- 4 slices bread
- olive oil

Add the banana, cornstarch, milk, salt, cinnamon, nutmeg, and nutritional yeast, if using, to a blender. The nutritional yeast will add a cheesy flavor.

Blend until smooth.

Put the bread in a casserole dish, and pour the banana mixture over it. Turn the slices to ensure both sides are coated. Let them soak for a few minutes.

Heat a little olive oil in a skillet over medium-high heat, and fry the bread slices for a few minutes on each side, until golden brown.

Pancakes

In Japan once I ordered pancakes at an American chain restaurant and watched as the chef pulled golden-brown disks out of the freezer and popped them in the microwave. No amount of high-fructose corn syrup could make them palatable. The pancakes in this recipe are lighter and fluffier than anything you'll get at a chain restaurant in this country or abroad. Put a little Earth Balance on top, and pour on the maple syrup.

- 1 cup all-purpose flour
- 2 teaspoons sugar
- 1 tablespoon baking powder
- ⅛ teaspoon salt
- 1 cup soy milk or nut milk
- 2 tablespoons canola oil or olive oil

Heat a wide skillet on the stovetop to medium-high.

In a large bowl, combine the flour, sugar, baking powder, and salt.

Add the soy milk and oil and stir until combined.

Scoop ½ cup of batter onto the skillet for each pancake, leaving a little space between them.

When you see bubbles in the middle of the pancake, flip it over.

The pancake is ready when the edges are firm.

TIMING

The chemistry of vegan cooking is sometimes very different from traditional methods. This recipe has the skillet heating up as you mix the ingredients. If the batter sits for too long, it will become foamy. That doesn't mean it's ruined, but it works best if cooked promptly after mixing.

Muesli

Not everyone would be excited about a recipe "developed by a Swiss nutritionist in the nineteenth century," but muesli really is the bomb. The advantage over granola is the absence of sugar or other sweeteners—these ingredients are naturally sweet and flavorful without it. Don't be scammed into buying muesli with corn flakes, chocolate drops, or other processed foods in it; real muesli comprises whole foods. The basics are always rolled oats, dried fruit, and nuts. Add fresh fruit in any proportion. Sliced apples are especially compatible.

- 2 cups old-fashioned oats (see the introduction on page 22)
- 1 cup unsalted nuts, such as whole almonds, slivered or sliced almonds, sunflower seeds, pecans, and walnuts
- ½ cup dried fruit, such as raisins, blueberries, cranberries, dates, and apricots
- soy milk or nut milk
- lemon juice (optional)

Mix all the ingredients together.

In a serving bowl, cover ½ cup of muesli with soy milk or nut milk and allow to soak for at least 10 minutes.

If desired, add a splash of lemon juice, the way Dr. Bircher-Benner did back in the old country.

Add fresh fruit, such as apples, bananas, sliced strawberries, and other berries.

Store dry muesli in a sealed container.

⇒ COMMERCIAL MUESLI

Almost as good as concocting your own version is Bob's Red Mill muesli, which is widely distributed in supermarkets and can be purchased online.

Fruit Smoothie

This is one of those recipes that requires a high-speed blender—otherwise the smoothie just won't be smooth. Use your favorite combination of fruits, with strawberries and apples as the base, and if you're feeling adventurous, throw in a handful of spinach leaves or lettuce. The flavor won't change much, but the color may be alarming. One sip, however, and you'll be sold, and the bump in nutrition is worth it.

1 cup strawberries, tops left on

½ apple, cored and seeded

1 cup water

TWO OR THREE OF:

½ cup blueberries

½ cup raspberries

½ cup pineapple chunks

½ navel orange

½ cup grapes

1 kiwi, peeled

other fruit of your choice

Combine all the ingredients in a high-speed blender and blend until smooth, about 20 seconds.

⇒ SOME LIKE IT COLD

Instead of water, throw in a cup of ice cubes for a thicker, slushy smoothie.

⇒ APPLES

Scientific research consistently tells us that consuming white fruit like apples has multiple health benefits. I make it a habit to throw some apple in a smoothie or munch on one every day. One of the most used tools in my kitchen is the apple corer, a simple press that takes out the core and splits the fruit into segments. It makes the apple-a-day habit nearly effortless.

Tofu Scramble

Tofu takes on the flavors of whatever you cook it with, and this recipe makes a hearty hot breakfast. In The Desert Rats, *Ned says that this dish feeds the soul as it fills the belly. Of course, as a nontheist, he's speaking metaphorically, meaning it will improve your emotional state. Put it on toast and have some fruit on the side.*

16 ounces (1 package) tofu

¼ cup nutritional yeast

½ teaspoon turmeric

½ teaspoon black salt

1 teaspoon olive oil

½ small onion, diced

½ red or yellow bell pepper, diced

½ cup spinach, chopped (optional)

½ teaspoon dried parsley

Combine the tofu, nutritional yeast, turmeric, and salt in a blender or food processor, and mix until smooth. Set aside.

Heat the olive oil in a skillet over medium-high heat and add the onion and bell pepper. Sauté until the onion is translucent, 2 or 3 minutes.

Add the tofu mixture to the skillet. Stir in the spinach, if using, and the parsley.

Cook the tofu, stirring constantly, until enough of the liquid cooks off to give it a pleasing scrambled texture.

⇒ BLACK SALT

Used in South Asian cooking, black salt has a high sulfur content, so it will give this dish an eggy aroma. If that's not for you, ordinary salt works fine in this recipe.

Starters

Guacamole

A lot of the flavor of guacamole is in the quality of the avocados. They are a fragile entity, too hard to use for days on end and then suddenly over-ripe, with a brief window of usability between. See the tip about buying avocados on page 101. You can adjust the quantities of any of the other ingredients in this recipe, and omit the cilantro if you're not a fan.

2 ripe avocados

1 tablespoon diced onion

1 tablespoon diced tomato

½ teaspoon lime juice

¼ teaspoon cayenne pepper

handful of cilantro leaves

salt

Cut open the avocados and remove the pits. With a spoon, scoop the contents into a medium bowl, and mash with a fork.

Add the remaining ingredients, mixing with the fork.

Serve with crudités—sliced bell peppers, celery stalks, and carrots—or corn chips.

TIMING

Don't make guacamole until close to the time you want to eat it—avocado starts to turn brown as soon as it's exposed to air. If you want to try to preserve the leftovers, put plastic wrap directly onto the surface of the guacamole, with no air space.

Quesadillas

Ned makes these cashew-cheese quesadillas in The Desert Rats *to cheer up his friend Gilbert, a vegan skeptic who considers microwave burritos to be haute cuisine. The quesadillas are so good that Gilbert is soon on board with Ned's cooking. These simple, hearty, and delicious Mexican treats are best complemented with crudités or a side salad of crunchy romaine.*

4 flour tortillas

1 batch of nacho cheese sauce (page 120) or cashew cheese sauce (page 119)

When making the cheese sauce, cook it long enough to make the sauce quite thick, and let the sauce cool for a few minutes to thicken further.

In a dry skillet, cook a tortilla over medium-high heat until it puckers slightly, about 1 minute.

Using a lifter, flip the tortilla over and cook the other side.

Spoon ¼ cup of the cheese sauce onto one side of the tortilla, spreading it evenly over one half of the tortilla.

Fold the tortilla in half over the cheese filling.

Cook for a minute, until the tortilla browns slightly. Carefully flip the quesadilla over to brown the other side.

Allow the quesadilla to cool for a minute, and cut into wedges.

⇒ QUANTITIES

The cheese recipes make enough to create 6 to 10 quesadillas, but this recipe makes only 4. Each quesadilla takes a few minutes in the skillet, and unless you want to eat in shifts, cooking more than 4 means the first one will be getting cold by the time you're finishing the last one.

Hummus

Hummus can be made with dried garbanzos (see the note on page 60) or canned. Dry beans taste better, in my mind, but it takes advance planning and more time. Using canned has the added advantage of providing aquafaba—the liquid the garbanzos are packed in. Keep the aquafaba when you drain the garbanzos and use it to make an amazing meringue (see page 96).

- ½ cup dry garbanzos, or 1 can garbanzos, rinsed
- ¼ teaspoon baking soda (optional)
- 1 garlic clove
- 1 tablespoon fresh parsley, chopped
- 3 tablespoons olive oil, plus more to garnish
- 2 tablespoons water
- 1 tablespoon lemon juice
- ¾ teaspoon salt
- ¼ teaspoon pepper

WITH DRY GARBANZOS

Soak the garbanzos under at least two inches of water. To make smooth and creamy hummus, stir the baking soda into the soaking water. Without the baking soda, the end product will have more texture.

Rinse the soaked garbanzos. In a saucepan, cover the garbanzos with fresh water and bring to a boil.

Reduce the heat and simmer for an hour.

Drain and rinse the beans.

WITH CANNED GARBANZOS

Drain the beans, reserving the liquid if you want to make meringue (see page 96), and rinse them under running water.

MAKING THE HUMMUS

Put all the ingredients in a food processor and blend until smooth, scraping down the sides once or twice to incorporate everything. Alternately, mash with a potato masher or a fork.

Garnish with olive oil and serve with crudités: celery sticks, sliced bell peppers, or, as Mason and Peggy do in *Billy Blood,* with those delicious mini peppers cut in half.

Veggie Pâté

Popularized in Quebec in the hippie era, "végé-pâté" goes well with crudités or crackers. At a party or a potluck, this dish makes a more exotic contribution than hummus or guacamole. The list of ingredients might seem long, but putting it all together goes quickly.

- 1 cup sunflower seeds
- 1 potato, peeled and roughly chopped
- 1 large carrot, roughly chopped
- 1 medium onion, roughly chopped
- 1 celery stalk, roughly chopped
- 1 garlic clove, minced
- 1½ cups water
- ½ cup flour
- ½ cup nutritional yeast
- ½ cup olive oil
- 2 teaspoons lemon juice
- ½ teaspoon thyme
- ½ teaspoon basil
- ½ teaspoon sage
- ½ teaspoon black pepper
- ½ teaspoon mustard powder
- ½ teaspoon salt

Preheat the oven to 350°F.

Lightly grease an 8-inch square baking dish.

Combine all the ingredients in a food processor and mix until smooth.

Transfer to the baking dish and bake for 1 hour, or until the pâté is bubbling and beginning to brown.

Tabbouleh

It takes some time to make this recipe, but it's mostly soaking and draining time. You can use cracked wheat instead of bulgur, but it has to be soaked a little longer. The texture is more pleasing if the parsley, onions, and tomatoes are uniformly minced. Tabbouleh can be served chilled, but I like it better at room temperature.

1½ cups bulgur

1 bunch fresh parsley, dried and minced

4 green onions, white and green parts, minced

4 medium tomatoes, peeled (see below), seeded, and chopped

½ cup olive oil

½ cup lemon juice

2 teaspoons fresh mint, minced (optional)

salt

pepper

In a bowl, cover the bulgur with water and let it soak for an hour.

Drain the bulgur in a fine-mesh strainer, letting it stand for 30 minutes to drain completely.

Combine the bulgur with the other ingredients.

PEELING TOMATOES

The easiest way to get the skin off tomatoes is to bring a few inches of water in a saucepan to a boil, drop in the tomatoes, wait 20 seconds, and drain them. Wait for the tomatoes to cool, and the skins should slip off in your fingers.

Soups

Raw Tomato and Red Pepper Soup

Light and fresh, tomato and red pepper make an unexpected happy flavor combination. Ripe tomatoes are crucial—this is a good dish if you've just been to the farmers market, or in harvest season if you grow your own. Factory-farmed supermarket tomatoes will yield a substandard experience. This soup really does require a high-speed blender—there's no other way to get the ingredients adequately broken down.

- 3 large ripe tomatoes, cut into rough chunks
- 2 red bell peppers, seeded and cut into chunks
- ½ teaspoon salt

Place all the ingredients in a high-speed blender. Blend until very well combined, about 1 minute.

Gazpacho

In Rubber Band Ball, *Peggy learns how to make a real gazpacho, focusing on mincing the cucumber in an aesthetically pleasing way. This hearty soup is a great way to use up a stale baguette or loaf of bread.*

- ½ loaf of bread
- 1 cucumber, cut into chunks
- 4 large ripe tomatoes
- ½ bell pepper, any color
- 1 celery stalk, chopped
- ½ sweet onion, quartered
- 2 garlic cloves
- 1 tablespoon lemon juice
- 3 tablespoons red wine vinegar or balsamic vinegar
- ¾ teaspoon salt
- ⅛ teaspoon black pepper
- 1 teaspoon chopped fresh parsley
- 1 teaspoon chopped fresh basil
- ¼ teaspoon cayenne pepper (optional)
- 1 tablespoon olive oil

Place the bread in a large bowl and add just enough water to saturate ¼ of the bread. Set it aside to soak in for about 15 minutes.

Finely dice about one-fifth of the cucumbers, tomatoes, bell pepper, celery, and onion.

Combine the remaining vegetables and the garlic, lemon juice, red wine vinegar or balsamic vinegar, salt, and pepper in a blender or food processor and process until smooth.

Pour the soup into a serving bowl, stir in the diced vegetables, parsley, and basil, and refrigerate for at least 30 minutes.

Serve with bread (see page 88) or croutons (see page 49).

CONSISTENCY

The thickness of the soup can be modified by how long you blend it. For a very thin soup, skip the dicing step above and blend all of the vegetables.

Parsnip Pearl Barley Soup

In Rubber Band Ball, *Ned makes his Aunt Alma's pearl barley soup, a household favorite. The flavors of this soup are surprisingly rich and complex, considering it has so few ingredients.*

2 parsnips, diced

3 medium carrots, diced

3 celery stalks, diced

1 medium onion, diced

1 cup split peas

1 cup lentils

10 cups water

½ cup pearl barley

In a large saucepan over medium heat, sauté the parsnips, carrots, celery, and onion until translucent, about four minutes.

Add the split peas, lentils, and water, and bring to a boil.

Immediately reduce the heat and simmer for 1 hour.

Blend the soup in a blender or with an immersion blender.

Add the pearl barley, and simmer for 1 hour.

MIREPOIX

Part of the magic of this soup is in the combination of carrot, celery, and onion, a common base for sauces and soups in French cooking called mirepoix. Traditional mirepoix is made with one part carrot, one part celery, and two parts onion. Browning vegetables adds a different flavor profile, but cooking them without browning them, as in this recipe, adds sweetness and the subtle flavors that mirepoix is known for.

Salads

Spicy Cucumber Salad

Delicious on a hot day, cucumbers deserve their reputation as cool. The jalapeño or red pepper in this recipe will also cool you off in the heat—it may sound counterintuitive, but it works. Reduce the amount of spice if you want a calmer experience.

- 4 cucumbers, sliced thinly
- 1 red bell pepper, sliced thinly
- ½ sweet onion, sliced thinly
- ½ jalapeño pepper, seeds removed, diced, or 1 teaspoon red pepper flakes
- 1 tablespoon lime juice
- 1 teaspoon salt
- 2 tablespoons granulated sugar
- ⅓ cup rice vinegar
- ½ teaspoon toasted sesame oil
- 2 teaspoons sesame seeds

Place all the sliced vegetables in a large bowl.

In a small bowl, mix the lime juice, salt, sugar, vinegar, and sesame oil.

Pour the mixture over the vegetables, add the sesame seeds, and toss well.

Chill in refrigerator for at least 30 minutes, and toss again before serving.

❋ SPEED THINGS UP WITH A MANDOLINE

A mandoline is an inexpensive kitchen gadget that makes short work of slicing lots of vegetables, as in this salad. You can adjust the thickness of the slices it makes, and some even have interchangeable blades to make julienne strips.

Tofu Caprese Salad

Ned tried growing tomatoes on the balcony one summer in Signs Point to Yes, *and he had such good luck that he came up with several creative ways to prepare them. Ned marinated his tofu, but that's not necessary—in this recipe, the simple flavors of tomato and basil are enough; the tofu takes on those flavors. Kosher salt has larger grains, which only matters for aesthetic reasons; table salt will taste the same. Freshly ground pepper is also aesthetically pleasing and adds texture and aroma.*

This salad is illustrated on Mason's desk on the cover of this book.

½ block tofu

1 large or 2 medium ripe tomatoes

8–10 fresh basil leaves

olive oil

kosher salt

freshly ground black pepper

Pat the tofu dry with a clean kitchen towel.

Cut the tofu into ¼-inch slices. Cut the tomato into similar ¼-inch slices.

On a plate, arrange the slices vertically in repeating order: tomato, tofu, and a basil leaf.

Drizzle the top with olive oil and season with salt and pepper.

⇒ TOMATOES

Factory-grown supermarket tomatoes these days are lovely and red, and surely retain their visual beauty when shipped across the country, but they are usually mealy and taste like wet cardboard. If you can't grow your own, the other options to obtain edible tomatoes are getting them at a farmers market, or buying an expensive premium supermarket product usually labeled "heirloom tomatoes."

Croutons

Croutons are an excellent garnish for caesar salad (illustrated together on page 50) and add a bit of crunch to soups like the raw tomato and red pepper soup (page 40). Traditionally croutons are made from a plain white bread like focaccia or an old baguette, or even the crusty bread in this book (page 88). Stale bread is easier to work with; you can leave fresh bread out overnight under a dish towel to dry out.

- 4 slices of bread
- 3 tablespoons olive oil
- 1 teaspoon garlic powder
- ½ teaspoon parsley, oregano, or a combination
- ½ teaspoon salt

Preheat the oven to 400°F.

Cut the bread into cubes.

In a medium bowl, toss together the cubes, oil, garlic powder, herbs, and salt, until the cubes are well coated.

Spread the cubes on a parchment paper–lined baking sheet and bake for about 5 minutes. Stir the cubes and bake for another 7 minutes or until golden brown.

⇾ OLIVE OIL

Rather than canola oil, I use olive oil for sautéing and to cook everything that requires a basic oil. You'll read dozens of scientific claims about the dangers of corn, canola, and olive oils, and the superior nutritional content of each. It seems like the jury is still out, but my thinking is that olive oil is part of the Mediterranean diet, which has statistically significant health benefits. If you're concerned about the various scandals over diluted and counterfeit European olive oil exports, it's not difficult to buy California olive oil. A nutty California extra-virgin olive oil is especially nice in this recipe. California olive oil might cost a little more, but your health is worth the investment.

Caesar Salad

In Rubber Band Ball, *Peggy uses an entire bulb of garlic to make the dressing for this caesar, and it does pack a powerful garlicky punch. If it seems too pungent, put the dressing in the fridge overnight, and the garlic will mellow out. Garlic preserved in a jar isn't a good substitute for this recipe—it really needs the flavor of fresh garlic.*

⅓ cup slivered almonds

5 garlic cloves

¾ cup tofu

¼ cup olive oil

3 tablespoons lemon juice

1 tablespoon red miso

1 tablespoon nutritional yeast

1 teaspoon granulated sugar

½ teaspoon mustard powder

2 medium heads romaine lettuce

Put the almonds in a food processor or blender and grind until crumbly.

Blend the other ingredients (except the lettuce) in a food processor or blender until smooth and creamy.

Stir in the ground almonds.

Chop the lettuce and mix well with the dressing.

Serve with croutons (page 49), if desired.

SWEETNESS

You can replace the sugar with ½ teaspoon agave syrup.

Rationalist Dressing

Versions of this dressing have been floating around since 1923, when a San Francisco chef named it after a popular play, The Green Goddess. *In keeping with Ned's nontheist ideas, this version of green goddess dressing involves no supernatural entities.*

½ cup tahini

½ cup apple cider vinegar

¼ cup tamari

1 tablespoon lemon or lime juice

3 garlic cloves

½ cup water

2 tablespoons dried parsley

1 tablespoon agave nectar or maple syrup

½ cup canola or olive oil

Add all the ingredients except the oil to a blender or food processor and puree until smooth and creamy.

With the blender running, slowly add the oil until it is well integrated. Add more water, a few teaspoons at a time, if you want a thinner consistency.

TAMARI VERSUS SOY SAUCE

Why tamari instead of soy sauce? The taste difference is indistinguishable, but tamari has just three simple ingredients, while soy sauce usually includes a long list of unpronounceable chemicals. Read more about tamari on page 14.

Sweet Mustard Dressing

This is a recipe that really does require a high-speed blender. A regular blender will leave lumps of garlic and won't adequately emulsify the oil and vinegar. This recipe makes about 8 ounces of dressing.

3½ tablespoons lemon juice

1 tablespoon apple cider vinegar

⅓ cup agave nectar

⅓ cup olive oil

2½ tablespoons spicy brown mustard

½ teaspoon salt

1 garlic clove

black pepper

Combine all ingredients in a high-speed blender and blend until smooth.

AGAVE

In the same genus as the plants used to make *mezcal* and tequila, agave is a desert succulent that yields delicious sweet nectar. It's actually sweeter than cane sugar, but the claims that it is in any way healthier than cane sugar are misleading; its nutrition profile and glycemic load are probably more akin to corn syrup, which is currently vilified as a root cause of the obesity epidemic. In cooking, agave is a great substitute for honey, however, which isn't vegan.

Asian Ginger Dressing

This recipe will become velvety smooth in a high-speed blender, and in a regular blender will have a bit of texture and will require a good shake before pouring.

½ cup rice wine vinegar

¼ cup olive oil

1 ½-inch piece ginger, peeled, or 1 tablespoon ginger powder

2 garlic cloves

1 tablespoon tamari

1 tablespoon sesame oil

1 tablespoon sambal oelek or 1 teaspoon red pepper flakes

1 teaspoon agave

Combine all the ingredients in a blender and blend until smooth.

Creamy Italian Dressing

This is a recipe that really does require a high-speed blender. A regular blender will leave lumps of garlic and won't adequately emulsify the oil and water. Use this standard herby dressing on any kind of lettuce, or as a dip for crudités.

⅔ cup raw cashews

½ cup water

⅓ cup lemon juice

½ teaspoon garlic powder or 1 garlic clove

2 teaspoons onion powder

1 teaspoon salt

⅓ cup olive oil

2 teaspoons parsley

2 teaspoons basil

1 teaspoon oregano

Add the cashews, water, lemon juice, garlic, onion powder, and salt to a high-speed blender and puree until smooth and creamy.

With the blender running, slowly add the oil until it is well integrated. Add more water, a few teaspoons at a time, if you want a thinner consistency.

Add the parsley, basil, and oregano, blending just long enough to integrate the herbs.

Mains

Pesto on Zucchini Noodles

With so much raw garlic, pesto packs a powerful punch, so rather than using it as a dip, it's usually served as a sauce for pasta, or in this case, zucchini noodles—think fewer calories and better nutrition. But you'll need a spiralizer to make the noodles from the vegetable. If you don't have one, go ahead and boil up some pasta.

PESTO

1½ cups fresh basil leaves

⅓ cup olive oil

1 cup raw almonds

5 garlic cloves

⅓ cup nutritional yeast

¾ teaspoon salt

½ teaspoon black pepper

NOODLES

2 or 3 large zucchini

PESTO

Combine all ingredients in a food processor or blender until the nuts are ground. Pesto should have some texture and not be completely smooth.

NOODLES

With a spiralizer, cut the zucchini into medium-size noodles.

Carefully drop the raw noodles into a stock pot of boiling water and turn off the heat, letting them sit submerged for 3 minutes.

Drain the noodles promptly; left in the water too long, they quickly go from just cooked to mushy.

In a large bowl, combine the pesto and the hot noodles, tossing with a pair of forks.

⇒ THE NUTS

Traditionally pesto is made with pine nuts, but many people find that something in pine nuts messes up their taste buds, making everything else taste metallic for a while. Almonds provide the right texture for pesto, but walnuts are another option, as they provide a similar flavor to the original. Cashews work too, for a creamier consistency.

Teriyaki Tofu

This teriyaki is probably not very authentic to Japanese cuisine, but the flavors make a delightful light main dish. Serve it with a side of steamed broccoli or other green vegetable.

TERIYAKI SAUCE

¾ cup water

1 tablespoon cornstarch

¼ cup tamari

2 tablespoons agave or sugar

1 tablespoon sesame oil

1 tablespoon mirin (see page 72) or white wine

1 tablespoon grated onion

1 garlic clove, minced

1 teaspoon lemon juice or lime juice

1 teaspoon grated fresh ginger, or ½ teaspoon ground ginger

TERIYAKI TOFU

16 ounces (1 package) firm tofu

1 tablespoon olive oil

1 tablespoon sesame seeds

TERIYAKI SAUCE

In a saucepan over medium-high heat, heat the water and cornstarch, whisking until steaming and breaking up the lumps.

Add the remaining ingredients and cook until the sauce thickens, stirring constantly, about 3 minutes.

TERIYAKI TOFU

Cut the tofu into ¾-inch cubes and place in a bowl with the teriyaki sauce, submerging as much as possible. Marinate for at least an hour, or as long as overnight in the refrigerator.

Over medium-high heat, heat olive oil in a skillet.

Add the tofu to the skillet, along with the marinade.

Cook for a few minutes, flipping once or twice with a spatula, until the tofu browns and the teriyaki thickens.

Garnish with the sesame seeds.

SPICE

To give the dish some heat, add ¼ to ½ teaspoon ground cayenne, or 1 tablespoon sambal oelek—a delightful Indonesian hot sauce that can be made with shrimp or fish, but the Huy Fong brand commonly found in this country is vegan and has a short list of ingredients. Sambal oelek is similar to sriracha sauce, but garlickier and chunkier and not loaded with sugar.

Socca

Originating on the Mediterranean coast of Italy and France around Genoa, socca is unleavened and made with garbanzo flour. Cory is a socca whiz and has provided a list of mix-ins that work extremely well.

Garbanzo flour is denser than wheat flour and has a bit of an earthy, nutty taste. You can mix the veggies or spices into the batter itself or put them on top, pizza-style. If you like your glutens living free and wild, this dough is for you!

- 1 cup garbanzo flour
- 1 cup water
- 1½ tablespoons olive oil, plus more for the pan
- ½ teaspoon salt
- ½ cup diced fruit or vegetable mix-ins, such as sun-dried tomatoes, olives, figs, herbs, mushrooms, chilies, orange slices, peach slices, onions, garlic, shallots, artichokes, pesto, or nuts

Mix the flour, water, olive oil, salt, and diced mix-ins together in a bowl. Set aside for 30 minutes. The flour will fully absorb the water.

Preheat the oven to 450°F.

Oil an oven-safe skillet and pour in the batter. A 10-inch cast-iron skillet works well for this recipe.

Cook the socca for 5 to 8 minutes or until the top begins to brown.

Slice and serve warm.

GARBANZOS

Known as chickpeas in some places and definitely garbanzos in the Southwest, you can also find garbanzo flour in Indian supermarkets, where it's called besan. If you have a high-speed blender, you can turn dried garbanzos into flour yourself. Used as flour, garbanzos have slightly less carbs than wheat flour but way more fiber, along with good quantities of calcium, potassium, magnesium, and even iron.

Thin-Crust Pizza with Sliced Red Peppers

Don't be put off by the thought of making your own pizza crust—it's relatively simple, and unlike making pastry, it doesn't take any special techniques or finesse. You do need a pizza stone to make it optimally crispy, but a metal pizza pan or baking sheet will work too.

TOPPING

1 red bell pepper

½ small onion (optional)

PIZZA DOUGH

1½ teaspoons active yeast, or one ¼-ounce yeast packet

¼ teaspoon granulated sugar

¾ cup warm water

1¾ cups all-purpose flour

½ teaspoon salt

ASSEMBLY

marinara sauce (optional; see the note on the facing page)

olive oil

TOPPING

Remove the seeds and ribs from the bell pepper.

Slice the pepper as thinly as possible, longitudinally rather than into rings.

Slice the onion as thinly as possible.

PIZZA DOUGH

Preheat the oven to 450°F.

Dissolve the yeast and the sugar in the water, and set aside for 8 minutes.

In a medium bowl, combine the flour and salt.

Pour the yeast and water mixture into the flour and mix well with a wooden spoon or your hands. Wear vinyl kitchen gloves if you don't want the dough directly on your hands.

→

Flip the dough out onto a floured surface and knead for two minutes.

Cut parchment paper to fit the pizza stone, pizza pan, or baking sheet. If you don't have parchment paper, lightly oil the surface of the stone or pan.

Form the dough into a ball and put it in the center of the parchment paper. Working from the middle outward, press the dough toward the edge of the paper, making it as thin as possible.

ASSEMBLY

With a spoon, spread a thin layer of marinara on the crust, if using. If not, brush the surface with olive oil, and arrange the onions (if using) and peppers on the surface in a single layer.

Bake for 10 to 12 minutes or until the edges of the crust are golden brown.

CRISPY CRUST

With this thin crust, the thinner the toppings, the crispier the crust will be. If the toppings are piled high, the crust will be mushy toward the middle. With this pizza, less is definitely more.

MARINARA

Marinara is a basic tomato sauce, usually containing only olive oil and tomatoes, and maybe a little basil. Good basic marinara can be purchased in jars, but make sure it doesn't contain added sugar or a bunch of chemicals. Alternately, make your own with the tomato sauce recipe on page 117.

Baked Eggplant

This dish is reminiscent of a traditional lasagna, but without the noodles. If you think eggplant is boring, the rich deliciousness of this dish will blow your mind. It's even better warmed up the second day.

VEGETABLES

1 large eggplant, cut lengthwise into thin slices

2 medium zucchini, cut lengthwise into thin slices

TOMATO SAUCE

2 tablespoons olive oil

3 green onions, diced

3 garlic cloves, chopped

2 ripe medium tomatoes, chopped, or 1 can diced tomatoes

2½ cups crumbled tempeh

¼ cup water

6 sun-dried tomatoes, chopped

2 tablespoons tomato paste

1 teaspoon ground cumin

½ teaspoon smoked paprika

salt

Preheat the oven to 375°F.

VEGETABLES

In a skillet, fry the eggplant and zucchini slices until soft, and set aside.

TOMATO SAUCE

In a skillet, heat the olive oil over medium-high heat. Add the green onions and fry until translucent. Add the garlic and cook for another minute.

Add the tomatoes and their liquid, and cook for about 2 minutes, stirring.

Add the remaining ingredients and simmer for about 10 minutes, stirring, until the sauce thickens. Remove from the heat.

CHEESE SAUCE

2 cups soy milk or nut milk (see the note on page 120)

3 tablespoons olive oil

3 tablespoons nutritional yeast

1 tablespoon flour

1 tablespoon Earth Balance or vegan butter

1 teaspoon vegan soup base or ½ vegan stock cube

½ teaspoon garlic powder

¼ teaspoon turmeric

salt

ASSEMBLY

½ cup vegan shredded cheese (optional)

olive oil, for drizzling

¼ teaspoon paprika

CHEESE SAUCE

In a saucepan over medium-high heat, combine all the ingredients, whisking constantly until the sauce thickens. Remove from the heat.

ASSEMBLY

Grease a rectangular oven dish with olive oil.

Line the bottom and sides with half the eggplant slices, overlapping a little.

Add a layer of the tomato sauce, then half the zucchini slices, and then half the cheese sauce.

Layer the remaining ingredients, finishing with the cheese sauce.

Drizzle the top with olive oil, dust with paprika, and sprinkle with the shredded cheese, if using.

Bake for 40 minutes. Let cool for 15 minutes before serving.

⇒ PAPRIKA AND HEAT

The smoked paprika used here creates a Middle Eastern grilled-eggplant flavor. If you're not a fan of smoky flavors, use regular paprika instead. Add ¼ teaspoon ground chipotle or cayenne pepper for some heat.

Mac and Cheese

Mac and cheese evokes memories of childhood for many, and in The Desert Rats, *Ned cannily prepares it for a friend as comfort food. The cheese sauce in this recipe is rich and creamy, but for a lighter sauce, you can substitute the simpler cashew cheese that appears on page 119.*

- 1 cup raw cashews
- 3 cups soy milk or nut milk (see the note on page 120)
- ½ cup canola oil or olive oil
- ½ cup nutritional yeast
- ¼ cup miso
- 3 tablespoons cornstarch
- 2 tablespoons lemon juice
- 2 teaspoons onion powder
- 1 teaspoon garlic powder
- ½ teaspoon white pepper
- ½ teaspoon salt
- 16 ounces macaroni noodles, cooked according to package directions
- panko crumbs (optional)

If you don't have a high-speed blender, cover the cashews in ½ inch of water and soak for at least two hours, then drain. (If they aren't soaked, a standard blender will produce a grainy sauce.)

In the blender, add all the ingredients except the noodles, and blend until smooth.

In a large saucepan over high heat, bring the cheese sauce to a boil, whisking constantly.

When the sauce bubbles, reduce the heat to low and continue whisking until the sauce thickens.

Combine the sauce with the cooked noodles.

Optional: For a bit of crunch, spoon the mac and cheese into ramekins, sprinkle the top with panko crumbs, and broil in the oven for a minute or two, watching closely, until the panko takes on a golden toasty color.

⇒ LEFTOVERS

If you want to put some of this dish aside, store the sauce and noodles separately in the fridge. If combined, the noodles will absorb all the sauce, leaving the noodles dry. If that happens, they can be partially reanimated in a bit of unflavored soy milk or nut milk in a saucepan over medium heat.

White Bean Chili

Mason relishes this white bean chili in Reach for the Sky *when he finds leftovers in the fridge. The chili improves as the flavors have a chance to meld after a night in the refrigerator, if it lasts that long. Peggy and Ned made this dish as part of their "white meal" in* Billy Blood. *Part of the fun of chili is mixing in a variety ingredients, so feel free to add chopped tomatoes, diced celery, and even different kinds of beans (see the tip below).*

- 1½ cups dry navy beans
- 7 cups vegetable stock
- 1 large yellow onion, chopped
- 2 poblano peppers, chopped
- ½ jalapeño pepper, minced
- 3 garlic cloves, minced
- 2 teaspoons ground cumin
- 1 teaspoon ground coriander
- 1 teaspoon chili powder
- 1 teaspoon oregano
- ½ teaspoon salt
- ¼ cup lime juice

In a stock pot, place the beans and the vegetable stock, and bring to a boil.

Reduce the heat to low, and simmer for 90 minutes.

Add the onions, peppers, garlic, spices, and salt.

Simmer for another 30 minutes.

Stir in the lime juice just before serving.

 **BEANS**

More traditional chili uses pinto beans or kidney beans, but navy beans are flavorful and create a lovely aesthetic. Other beans will take more or less time to cook completely, so if you use another variety, check on the minimum cooking time. It's important for kidney beans, specifically, to be completely cooked to deactivate a natural toxin they contain.

You'll hear various opinions about whether beans need to be soaked ahead or not; if you're organized enough to remember to do that, go for it, but this dish is delicious whether the beans are soaked or not.

Curry

I can't really call this a Thai curry or an Indian curry, because it's neither. In Reach for the Sky, *Peggy enlists Mason's help in sorting out the proportions for the spices, and they came up with a good balance.*

- 1 tablespoon ground coriander
- 1 tablespoon ground cumin
- 1 tablespoon turmeric
- 1 teaspoon white pepper
- 3½ cups (2 cans) coconut milk
- 2 hot chili peppers, such as jalapeño or habanero, cut in half and seeded
- 3 garlic cloves
- 1 tablespoon grated fresh ginger
- handful of fresh cilantro leaves
- 3 cups of at least 3 veggies, such as:
  - broccoli, cut into evenly sized florets
  - fingerling potatoes, quartered
  - onions, cut into wedges
  - tomatoes, quartered
  - bok choy, cut into evenly sized pieces
  - mushrooms, sliced
  - firm tofu, cubed
  - bell peppers, chopped

Add the cumin, coriander, turmeric, and pepper to a dry skillet over medium-high heat and stir constantly. When they become aromatic, which happens quickly, remove from the heat.

Put the spices in a blender and add the coconut milk, chili peppers, garlic, ginger, and half the cilantro. Blend until smooth.

Transfer the curry to a saucepan and bring to a boil. Reduce the heat and simmer for 5 minutes.

In the microwave or a steamer, cook the vegetables until nearly fully cooked. They should be cooked but still have a little crispness.

Drain the veggies, place them in a serving bowl, and ladle the curry over them. Garnish with the remaining cilantro.

RICE

Curry goes well with rice. Jasmine rice is a traditional option, but short-grain sticky Calrose rice works well too. Another fun option is red rice, which has a nutty flavor and higher nutritional content than white rice.

Onion, Pepper, and Mushroom Hash

Peggy makes this hash and serves it over vegan dogs to cheer up one of Mason's clients in Rubber Band Ball. *It worked, because this recipe is delicious. Serve it over vegan sausages or hot dogs in hot dog buns, or on toast.*

- 1 tablespoon olive oil
- 1 large yellow onion, sliced vertically
- 1 red or yellow bell pepper, sliced
- 1 green bell pepper, sliced
- 1 cup sliced mushrooms
- 1 teaspoon chili powder
- ½ teaspoon ground chipotle pepper or ground cayenne pepper
- salt

Heat the olive oil in a skillet over medium-high heat.

Add the onions and cook, stirring, until translucent.

Add the peppers and cook, stirring, until they begin to soften.

Add the mushrooms and cook until soft. If the mixture is too dry, add 1 or 2 tablespoons water.

Add the chili powder, chipotle or cayenne, and salt, and cook for another minute.

⇒ HOT DOG TOPPING

This hash has a hot, smoky flavor from the chipotle, but to make it more like a traditional hot dog topping, instead of the chili powder and chipotle, mix in 2 tablespoons of tomato paste, 1 teaspoon of brown sugar or agave syrup, 1 tablespoon mustard, and 1 teaspoon tamari.

Cold Soba Noodles with Dipping Sauce

Traditionally eaten with chopsticks, soba noodles can also be twirled around a fork like pasta. Don't be afraid to pick up the dishes—it makes the dipping part easier and less messy.

- ¾ cup water
- 3 tablespoons tamari
- 2 tablespoons mirin, or 1 teaspoon sugar plus 1 tablespoon white wine, or 1 teaspoon sugar
- ½ teaspoon grated ginger
- 8 ounces soba noodles
- 1 green onion, both green and white parts, minced
- 1 tablespoon sesame seeds

Combine the water, tamari, mirin, and ginger, and stir to incorporate the sugar, if using. Divide the dipping sauce into two bowls.

Cook the soba noodles according to the package directions. Drain the noodles in a colander and rinse under cold running water until completely cool.

Let the noodles drain for a minute in the colander, then arrange on two plates.

Garnish the noodles with the green onion and the sesame seeds.

MIRIN

Mirin is a sweet Japanese cooking wine. It doesn't have a lot of alcohol in it, but because it has some, it's regulated like booze. It can be purchased in supermarkets that carry alcoholic beverages, but prepare to be carded at the register.

Roasted Squash

It might seem like a lot of work to turn a whole butternut squash into a meal, but this recipe is simple and quick. The only difficult part is cutting the squash in half—you need a large, very sharp chef's knife and some serious elbow grease.

1 butternut squash

1 teaspoon olive oil

2 tablespoons maple syrup

¼ teaspoon dill

¼ teaspoon ground thyme

¼ teaspoon ground sage

Preheat the oven to 400°F.

Wash the squash and cut in half lengthwise. Scoop out the seeds and discard.

Brush the inner surfaces with the olive oil.

Place the squash halves skin side down on a foil-lined baking sheet.

Roast for 45 minutes.

Test for doneness by sticking a fork into the squash. If the flesh is still too firm to be palatable, cook longer, in 5-minute increments.

Let the squash cool for 5 minutes.

Drizzle the inner surfaces with the maple syrup and sprinkle with the herbs.

Serve each half in a soup plate.

Cold Chinese Noodles with Sesame Sauce

This dish is easy to put together and is always a hit at a dinner party or as a contribution to a potluck. If you use wheat noodles, such as spaghetti, wait until just before serving to combine the sauce and the noodles. If left too long, the noodles will absorb all the sauce and the dish will seem dry.

SAUCE

- ½ cup tamari
- ¼ cup sesame oil
- 3 tablespoons rice vinegar
- 2 tablespoons chili oil
- 2 tablespoons peanut oil
- 2 tablespoons tahini
- 3 garlic cloves, crushed and minced
- 1 tablespoon ginger, diced
- 1 teaspoon granulated sugar or agave

ASSEMBLY

- 1 pound glass noodles or spaghetti noodles
- ½ cup green onions, white and green parts, chopped

In a medium bowl, whisk together all the sauce ingredients.

Cook the noodles according to the package directions. Rinse under running water to cool them. If you won't be using them right away, toss them with 1 tablespoon sesame oil to prevent them from sticking.

Just before serving, toss the noodles with the sauce and the green onions.

Vegan Ricotta and Spinach-Stuffed Shells

Ned makes this satisfying dish for Mason before he heads out on a ghost hunt in The Invisible Arrow. *Without the pasta the spinach and ricotta makes a great dip, or spread it on crackers as a snack.*

- 16 ounces giant pasta shells
- 2 teaspoons olive oil
- ½ cup cashews
- ½ cup nutritional yeast
- ¼ cup lemon juice
- 3 tablespoons vegetable stock or water
- 3 garlic cloves
- 16 ounces (1 package) firm tofu
- ½ cup fresh spinach, chopped
- 1 teaspoon parsley
- ½ teaspoon basil
- ½ teaspoon salt
- ½ cup marinara sauce

Preheat the oven to 350°F.

Cook the shells according to the package directions. After draining, toss gently with the olive oil, and set aside.

If you don't have a high-speed blender, cover the cashews in ½ inch of water and soak for at least two hours, then drain. (If they aren't soaked, a standard blender will produce a grainy sauce.)

In a high-speed blender, add the cashews, nutritional yeast, lemon juice, stock or water, and garlic. Blend until smooth.

In a food processor or large bowl, add the cashew liquid, tofu, spinach, spices, and salt, and mix until well combined.

Lightly grease a casserole dish.

With a spoon or spatula, scoop the ricotta into the shells. Arrange the shells in the casserole dish, open-side up.

Spoon marinara over the shells, not drenching them but leaving some of the pasta and ricotta exposed.

Bake for 20 minutes, or until the marinara is bubbly.

Seitan Stroganoff

Named for a nineteenth-century Russian diplomat, thick and hearty stroganoff is perfect for a winter evening meal. Steam some asparagus, which comes into season in February, to serve on the side, sprinkled with lemon juice.

- 1 tablespoon olive oil
- 1 onion, chopped
- 2 garlic cloves, minced
- 12 ounces seitan, cut into strips
- 4 cups sliced mushrooms
- 1 tablespoon lemon juice
- 1 teaspoon tarragon
- ½ teaspoon paprika
- 2 tablespoons tahini
- 2 cups vegetable stock
- 8 ounces fettucine noodles
- salt
- pepper
- 2 tablespoons fresh minced parsley, or 1 tablespoon dry parsley

Heat the oil in a large skillet over medium heat and add the onion and garlic, stirring until the onions are translucent.

Add the seitan and the mushrooms and stir, cooking until the mushrooms soften.

Add the lemon juice, tarragon, and paprika, and mix well.

Stir the tahini into the stock.

Stir the stock mixture into the mushroom mixture, and cook until the mixture thickens.

Cook the noodles according to the package directions.

Season the stroganoff with the salt and pepper, spoon over the noodles, and garnish with parsley.

Fried Tempeh with Plum Sauce

Fried tempeh works well served hot or at room temperature. Pair it with red peppers or string beans, or like Ned does in The Man from Grapalia, *alongside caesar salad.*

PLUM SAUCE

- 2 large or 3 small plums, including skins, pitted and chopped, or ½ cup plum jam
- 2 tablespoons vinegar
- 1 tablespoon brown sugar
- 1 tablespoon onion powder
- 1 teaspoon red pepper flakes
- 1 garlic clove, minced
- ½ teaspoon ground ginger

TEMPEH

- 8 ounces tempeh
- 2 tablespoons tamari
- 1 tablespoon olive oil

FOR SERVING

bell peppers, sliced and grilled (optional)

PLUM SAUCE

In a saucepan over medium heat, combine all the ingredients and bring to a boil.

Simmer until the fruit breaks down.

Allow the sauce to cool.

TEMPEH

Cut the tempeh into rectangles.

Sprinkle the tamari evenly over the tempeh pieces, letting it soak in.

In a skillet, heat the oil over medium-high heat.

Fry the tempeh pieces, turning regularly, until it takes on some golden color.

ASSEMBLY

Plate the tempeh, if desired tossing with grilled bell peppers slices.

Drizzle with the plum sauce.

PLUM JAM

If you use jam instead of fresh fruit, buy a brand without added sugar.

Seitan Wellington and Mushroom Gravy

This hearty dish is perfect for fall—rich and satisfying and dramatic enough for Thanksgiving dinner or a winter holiday meal. The mushroom gravy to pour over it appears on page 90.

1 package puff pastry (Pepperidge Farm frozen puff pastry is an incidentally vegan product) or 1 package phyllo sheets

VEGGIE FILLING

1 tablespoon olive oil

½ small onion, finely chopped

3 carrots, finely chopped

½ teaspoon dried thyme or 1 tablespoon fresh thyme leaves

¼ cup red wine

¼ teaspoon salt

¼ teaspoon black pepper

2 tablespoons flour

3 cups baby spinach leaves

Preheat the oven to 400°F.

VEGGIE FILLING

In a large sauté pan, heat the olive oil, add the onion and carrots, and cook for 5 minutes.

Add the thyme, red wine, salt, pepper, flour, and spinach, and cook for another 3 minutes.

→

PUFF PASTRY

In French cooking, puff pastry traditionally has butter in it, but there are a couple of vegan brands available, including, surprisingly, Pepperidge Farm frozen puff pastry. It's made by one of the mega factory food corporations and thus should be available in almost any supermarket in the land. You can also make your own puff pastry; several recipes can found online, including a good one from OneGreenPlanet.org.

SEITAN

3 cups seitan (about two boxes)

½ teaspoon dried thyme or 1 tablespoon fresh thyme leaves

2 tablespoons prepared mustard or 1 teaspoon mustard powder

2 tablespoons red wine

1 tablespoon maple syrup

¾ cup flour

1 teaspoon lemon zest

½ teaspoon smoked paprika

salt

pepper

SEITAN

In a food processor, combine all the ingredients in this section until uniformly mixed.

WELLINGTON

On a lightly floured surface, stretch out each sheet of puff pastry until it is about ¼ inch thick.

Divide the veggie filling among the sheets of pastry, leaving enough room at the edge of the sheet to fold it closed.

Divide the seitan mixture on top of the veggie filling.

Fold the puff pastry over to make a tube shape, and tuck in the ends.

Bake for 40 minutes, or until the pastry is golden brown.

Let rest 10 minutes before slicing.

Slather mushroom gravy (page 90) on top of each slice.

⇾ USING PHYLLO

Phyllo is harder to work with than puff pastry, but the delicate crispiness is hard to match. Use 3 to 5 sheets of phyllo for each Wellington roll. Two tips for working with phyllo: keep it under a damp cloth until you need to peel off the next sheet, and use a brush to gently put spread olive oil on each sheet. The oil makes the delicate pastry a little easier to work with, and it increases the deliciousness of the final product dramatically.

Tempeh Salad

Peggy served this tempeh salad as a main course, with crackers and sliced bell peppers, in Penstock Canyon. *It's also nice on toast. Even though there are a lot of ingredients, putting it together is quick and easy.*

- 8 ounces tempeh
- 1 stalk celery, finely chopped
- 3 green onions, white parts, finely chopped
- ¼ red bell pepper, finely chopped
- ¼ green bell pepper, finely chopped
- 2 tablespoons finely chopped onion
- 2 tablespoons sunflower seeds or chopped almonds (optional)
- 1 tablespoon finely chopped Italian or flat-leaf parsley
- ½ cup or more mayonnaise
- 2 tablespoons sweet relish
- 1 tablespoon tamari
- 1 tablespoon lemon juice
- ½ teaspoon minced fresh garlic
- ½ teaspoon ground cumin
- ½ teaspoon ground dill

Break up the tempeh and place it in a steamer basket. Steam for 15 minutes.

In a large bowl, combine the remaining ingredients. When they tempeh has cooled, mix it in.

If the mixture seems dry, add more mayonnaise.

Chill the salad in the refrigerator for an hour or longer before serving.

⇒ MAYONNAISE

There are several brands of vegan mayonnaise on the market, but the one I like best is Just Mayo, from a newish company founded specifically to make plant-based processed foods using Silicon Valley capital. In 2014 the largest processed food manufacturer on the planet, Unilever, sued to prevent Just Mayo being called mayonnaise, and lost; now Unilever makes its own vegan mayo. That's a victory for animal welfare and human health, but skip Unilever's mainstream Hellman's brand and find the Just Mayo—you'll love it.

Sides

Roasted Green Cauliflower Steaks

There's something special about green cauliflower (opposite)—this recipe doesn't work with white cauliflower or the lovely pink ones. The flavor is startling, melt-in-your-mouth rich and buttery, and doesn't taste anything like cauliflower.

1 head green cauliflower

olive oil

salt

Preheat the oven to 450°F.

Trim the leaves and stems. It's not necessary to completely remove the stems.

Slice the cauliflower from the top downward into ½-inch slices. Toward the sides, the florets will crumble into smaller pieces rather than slices. These cook up nicely; just make sure none are thicker than about ½ inch.

Brush both sides of the steaks and the smaller pieces with olive oil. Sprinkle with salt.

Arrange the cauliflower flat on a foil-lined baking sheet.

Bake for 13 minutes.

Remove from the oven, and turn each piece over. Brush with olive oil and sprinkle with salt.

Bake for another 13 minutes.

Crusty Bread

If you haven't made bread before, it's simpler than you might imagine. The best way to make bread with a crispy crust was revealed to the New York Times *in 2006 by chef Jim Lahey. I've tried misting the bread with water while it's baking, and putting a pan of water in the oven with the loaf, but Lahey's method is the only way that works well: the loaf is baked inside a preheated cast-iron Dutch oven.*

- 1 cup whole-wheat flour
- 2½ cups bread flour or all-purpose flour
- 1 teaspoon active yeast, or 1 yeast packet
- 1 teaspoon salt
- 1¾ cups water
- ½ cup cracked wheat or bulgur wheat (optional)
- cornmeal, for dusting

In a large bowl, combine the flours, yeast, and salt.

Add the cracked wheat, if desired, to give the final loaf some additional texture.

Mix in the water, and knead just until well-mixed and shaggy in texture.

Put plastic wrap over the bowl and let it rise for 2 or 3 hours, or even overnight. The loaf will double in size.

Heat the oven to 450°F.

Put a large cast-iron or enamel Dutch oven or pot that has a lid in the oven to heat for 30 minutes.

Remove the pot to the stovetop or a trivet. Sprinkle a thin layer of cornmeal over the bottom of the pot; it might smoke a little.

Without deflating the loaf, carefully tip it into the pot. Shake the pot if necessary to distribute the loaf evenly. Replace the lid, and put the pot in the oven.

Bake for 30 minutes. Remove the lid from the pot and bake for another 15 minutes, or until the loaf is golden brown.

Allow the loaf to cool on a rack.

1950s Peas and Carrots

Mason runs across this classic 1950s dish in The Invisible Arrow, *when it's the only vegan dish he can find. This simple recipe demonstrates how our Cold War predecessors ate their vegetables.*

- 2 large or 3 medium carrots, diced into ¼-inch cubes
- 8 ounces frozen green peas or 1 can green peas
- ¼ teaspoon salt
- ½ teaspoon lemon juice
- ½ heaping teaspoon granulated sugar or ½ teaspoon agave syrup (optional)

BOILING WATER

Fill a medium saucepan halfway with water and bring to a boil. Drop in the carrots and cook for 2 minutes.

If using frozen peas, add them to the water and cook for another 2 minutes, until the carrots are soft.

If using canned peas, cook the carrots for another 2 minutes, until soft. Strain the peas, discarding the liquid, and add them to the saucepan for 20 seconds.

Drain the vegetables and put them in a medium bowl. Stir in the salt and lemon juice, and for a real taste of the 1950s, the sugar or agave syrup.

MICROWAVE

Cook the cubed carrots in a covered dish for 1 or 2 minutes, until soft.

If using frozen peas, microwave the peas until soft.

If using canned peas, strain the peas, discarding the liquid.

In a medium bowl, combine the carrots and the peas. Stir in the salt and lemon juice, and for a real taste of the 1950s, the sugar or agave syrup.

Mushroom Gravy

Thick and rich, this gravy goes nicely over any vegetable and especially over seitan or tempeh. Cory says it's delicious on toast, as illustrated. Mushroom gravy is a key ingredient in Seitan Wellington (page 80).

- 1 small onion, minced
- 1 cup white mushrooms, chopped
- ¼ cup olive oil
- 2½ cups vegetable stock, divided
- 2 tablespoons tamari
- ¼ cup flour
- ½ teaspoon dried sage
- ½ teaspoon dried thyme
- ½ teaspoon dried marjoram
- 1 teaspoon black pepper
- 1 tablespoon nutritional yeast (optional)

In a large skillet, heat the olive oil and add the onions and mushrooms. Sauté over high heat for 2 minutes.

Reduce the heat and add 1½ cups of the vegetable stock and the tamari.

Put the flour in a small bowl and add the remaining 1 cup of the vegetable stock, whisking to combine.

Pour the flour mixture into the skillet and stir.

Bring to a low boil, and then reduce the heat.

Add the spices and nutritional yeast, stirring.

Cook for 8 to 10 minutes, until the gravy thickens.

FOR CREAMIER GRAVY

Pour half the gravy in a high-speed blender with 2 tablespoons raw cashews and blend until it's very smooth, then stir it into the unblended portion.

Atomic Pinto Beans

In The Invisible Arrow, *Mason worries that the pinto beans he's been served in a diner are contaminated by radioactive fallout. There hasn't been too much of that happening since the golden age of atmospheric atomic testing ended in 1963, with exceptions, of course, like Chernobyl, Fukushima, various Russian industrial accidents, and perhaps whatever the North Koreans are up to, but generally the beans we eat are probably fairly safe.*

- 1 cup dried pinto beans
- 1 tablespoon olive oil
- ½ onion, diced
- 2 garlic cloves, minced
- 1 large or 2 small tomatoes, diced, or 1 can diced tomatoes
- 1 teaspoon chili powder
- ½ teaspoon ground cayenne pepper, or 1 teaspoon red pepper flakes
- ½ teaspoon ground cumin
- ½ teaspoon salt

If you have time or plan well enough to soak the beans, put them in at least three cups of water in a covered pot or bowl and leave them overnight, up to 12 hours.

Drain the beans, if you soaked them, and rinse them in a colander.

Put the beans in a saucepan with four cups of water and bring to a boil. Reduce the heat to a simmer and cook for 1½ hours, if they were soaked, and up to 3 hours or longer, replenishing the water when needed. Test for doneness by fishing out a bean and rinsing it under the tap until it's cool, then biting into it. If it still has a mealy texture, it needs to cook longer.

Drain the beans and set aside.

Over medium-high heat in a deep skillet or large saucepan, heat the olive oil.

Add the onion and garlic and cook until translucent, stirring constantly.

Add the tomatoes, spices, and salt, and cook until the tomatoes start to break down.

Add the beans, and cook for another few minutes over medium heat, until the sauce thickens slightly.

⇒ CANNED TOMATOES

Putting food in sealed metal containers was a marvelous technological innovation in the nineteenth century that allowed people to eat green vegetables in winter and on long ocean voyages. It meant twentieth-century cooks could simply crank the can opener and dump the contents into a saucepan—voilà, dinner. It may sound heretical to the modern ear to include canned tomatoes in this recipe, but in truth tomatoes are one of the only vegetables that cans really well, and if your only other option is flavorless factory-grown fresh tomatoes (see the note on page 48), you might as well go for the can.

Desserts

Meringue Cookies

In 2015 a guy in Indiana named Goose Wohlt figured out that the liquid garbanzo beans are cooked in can be whipped into beautiful meringue. He perfected the technique and named the liquid aquafaba, from the Latin words for water and bean. It's incredibly simple to do and tastes lighter than the animal-product equivalent. If you don't like egg-white meringue, try this version anyway—it won't stick to your teeth the way egg white does, and it literally melts in your mouth.

liquid from one can of garbanzo beans (about ½ cup)

½ teaspoon cream of tartar (optional)

⅓ cup granulated sugar

Preheat the oven to 200°F.

Make sure the bowls and whisk are clean and dry. Any trace of oil will prevent the liquid from foaming properly.

Line two baking sheets with parchment paper.

Put the aquafaba in the bowl of a mixer, or in a large metal bowl. Sprinkle on the cream of tartar.

Use the mixer's whisk attachment, or a hand whisk, and beat until the resulting foam forms stiff peaks, about 10 minutes, adding the sugar halfway through.

Drop spoonfuls of the meringue onto the parchment paper, leaving a little space between them.

Bake for 90 minutes, then let the cookies cool completely.

⋙ TIMING

These cookies need to be enjoyed promptly, or sealed in an airtight container. If they sit out, they become gummy in a matter of hours. Happily they can be crisped up again in a warm oven if necessary.

Baked Doughnuts

This recipe requires doughnut pans. If you don't have those, you can form the dough into doughnut shapes with your hands, but it's messy; try wearing well-oiled vinyl food-prep gloves. Unlike the deep-fried variety found at strip malls, these doughnuts are rich and cakey.

DOUGHNUTS

- ½ cup nut milk or soy milk
- ½ teaspoon apple cider vinegar
- ½ teaspoon vanilla extract
- 4 tablespoons Earth Balance, vegan butter, or vegan shortening
- 1 cup all-purpose flour
- ½ cup granulated sugar
- 1 teaspoon baking powder
- ¼ teaspoon salt
- ¼ teaspoon grated nutmeg
- ¼ teaspoon cinnamon

GLAZE

- ½ cup powdered sugar
- 1 tablespoon nut milk or soy milk

Preheat the oven to 350°F.

In a saucepan, whisk together the nut milk or soy milk, vinegar, vanilla, and Earth Balance. Warm the mixture over low heat until it is warm to the touch but not hot.

In a large bowl, mix the flour, sugar, baking powder, salt, nutmeg, and cinnamon.

Add the milk mixture to the bowl and mix until just combined.

Pour the batter into doughnut pans and bake for 12 minutes, until the surface springs back when pressed.

While the doughnuts are cooling, whisk together the powdered sugar and nut milk or soy milk to make the glaze.

Tip the doughnuts out of the pans, and drizzle them with the glaze.

Peanut Butter Cookies

Take a batch of these as a gift when you're invited to someone's house. Even though they can be whipped up in under half an hour, your hosts will be impressed with your kitchen prowess.

- 1 cup all-purpose flour
- ½ cup fresh peanut butter (see the tip below)
- ½ cup granulated sugar
- ¼ cup brown sugar
- ¼ cup Earth Balance, vegan butter, or vegan shortening
- ¼ cup nut milk or soy milk
- 2 teaspoons lemon juice
- 2 teaspoons vanilla extract
- 1 teaspoon baking soda
- ½ teaspoon salt
- ¼ cup vegan chocolate chips (optional)
- ¼ cup pecan pieces (optional)

Preheat the oven to 350°F.

Place all ingredients, except the chocolate chips and pecan pieces, into a food processor or large bowl and blend until well combined.

Mix in the chocolate chips and pecan pieces, if using.

Line two baking sheets with parchment paper.

Roll the dough into 1-inch balls and flatten them with your hand on the baking sheet, spaced about 2 inches apart. The dough should make 15 or 20 cookies.

Bake for 10 minutes or until golden brown. Baking them a little longer will make them a lot crunchier.

Cool the cookies on wire racks.

⇒ BUYING PEANUT BUTTER

Many supermarket brands of peanut butter have lots of added sugar and a long list of chemical ingredients. Look for brands that have one ingredient: peanuts. Some stores sell their own freshly made peanut butter in the bulk section. It's a delicious whole food that doesn't need to be adulterated, and if you've been eating the processed stuff, you'll quickly notice how much better it is when made simply.

Oatmeal Cookies

Nothing says homemade like oatmeal cookies. These aren't overly sweet and will last for several days in a sealed container. Read about the types of oatmeal in the introduction on page 22.

1½ cups old-fashioned oats

1 cup flour

½ cup brown sugar

½ teaspoon baking soda

¼ teaspoon salt

¼ cup canola oil or coconut oil

¼ cup unsweetened applesauce

¼ cup water

Preheat the oven to 350°F.

Line two baking sheets with parchment paper.

In a large bowl, mix the oats, flour, sugar, baking soda, and salt.

Stir in the oil, mixing thoroughly.

Add the applesauce and water, stirring until well combined.

Transfer the dough to a floured surface. Using the lip of a drinking glass, cut out rounds. Gather the remaining dough and flatten it again, cutting out more rounds.

Arrange the rounds on the parchment paper, leaving space between them.

Bake for 12 minutes or until golden.

Cool completely.

Secret Avocado Chocolate Mousse

It might seem weird to use avocados as a base for a mousse, but the tendency for avocados to quickly turn brown when exposed to air isn't an issue with this treat. Unlike most things you make with avocados, this mousse will last for several days in the refrigerator.

4 ripe avocados, peel and pit removed

¼ cup coconut oil

1 cup unsweetened cocoa powder

1½ cups granulated sugar

¾ cup water

Place the avocados, oil, cocoa powder, and sugar in a high-speed blender or food processor and blend, adding the water a few tablespoons at a time until a palatable mousse consistency is reached.

BUYING AVOCADOS

Where I live in Southern California, the most flavorful avocados are sold by street vendors who get them from garden trees. Supermarket avocados are part of the factory food system, often shipped from hundreds of miles away. If you can't find soft ones, let them ripen on the counter for a day or two inside a paper bag with a banana.

Red Velvet Cake

Often claimed as Southern cuisine, the origins of red velvet cake are obscure, but the fun part is that the shocking red interior is concealed until you cut into the white icing.

CAKE

- 3½ cups flour
- 1½ cups granulated sugar
- 2 teaspoons baking soda
- 2 teaspoons unsweetened cocoa powder
- 1 teaspoon salt
- 2 cups soy milk or nut milk
- ⅔ cup canola oil
- 3 tablespoons red food coloring
- 2 tablespoons vinegar
- 2 teaspoons vanilla extract

CAKE

Preheat the oven to 350°F.

Lightly oil two 8-inch round cake pans.

In a large bowl, combine the flour, sugar, baking soda, cocoa powder, and salt, whisking to combine.

Add the soy milk or nut milk, oil, food coloring, vinegar, and vanilla, and mix until smooth.

Pour half the batter into each cake pan, and place in the oven.

Bake for 35 minutes and test for doneness by inserting a toothpick in the middle of the cake. If it comes out clean, the cake is done; if not, bake 5 minutes longer and test again.

Let the cakes cool for 10 minutes in the pans. Run a knife or spatula around the edges to loosen them, then invert the pans onto wire racks.

Let the cakes cool completely before frosting.

continued overleaf →

continued from page 102

FROSTING

- ¼ cup nondairy cream cheese
- ¼ cup Earth Balance, vegan butter, or vegan shortening, at room temperature
- ½ teaspoon vanilla extract
- 3 cups powdered sugar
- soy milk or nut milk, as needed

FROSTING

In the bowl of a food mixer or a large bowl, add the cream cheese and Earth Balance. Beat until fluffy, about 5 minutes.

Mix in the vanilla. Add the powdered sugar, ½ cup at a time, and beat until smooth.

If the frosting is too dry, add ½ teaspoon soy milk or nut milk and beat it in, using more if necessary. The frosting should be stiff, not runny.

ASSEMBLY

Tip one of the cakes onto a plate and apply the frosting with a spatula or knife, completely concealing the cake.

Tip the second layer on top and apply the frosting, making sure none of the red cake is visible.

Zucchini Bread

People in smaller communities joke about the glut of zucchini that happens at harvest time, and how everyone gives it away because there's too much of it to use. I don't know anyone in Los Angeles who has enough garden space to have a surplus of any vegetable, but even if you have to buy them, zucchini bread is a solid staple.

3 tablespoons ground flaxseed

¼ cup warm water

1 cup brown sugar

¼ cup canola oil

¼ cup unsweetened applesauce

½ teaspoon vanilla extract

2 medium zucchini, grated

1½ cups all-purpose or whole-wheat flour

2 teaspoons baking powder

¼ teaspoon baking soda

½ teaspoon cinnamon

1 teaspoon grated nutmeg

½ teaspoon salt

½ cup raisins (optional)

Preheat the oven to 350°F.

Grease a loaf pan with canola oil.

In a small bowl, mix the flaxseeds and the water.

In a large bowl, mix together the sugar, oil, applesauce, and vanilla.

Mix in the grated zucchini.

In a separate large bowl, mix together the flour, baking powder, baking soda, cinnamon, nutmeg, and salt.

Add the flour mixture to the zucchini mixture and stir just until everything is evenly combined. Fold in the raisins, if using.

Pour the batter into the loaf pan and bake for 50 minutes, or until a toothpick inserted into the center comes out clean.

Let the loaf cool for 10 minutes before running a spatula or knife around the sides of the pan. Invert the pan over a plate or cutting board to release the loaf.

Chocolate Layer Cake

If you're used to cakes with animal products, you'll find the taste of this chocolatey delight richer, more nuanced, and far superior to any traditional chocolate cake.

CAKE

- 2 cups all-purpose flour
- 1⅓ cups granulated sugar
- ⅓ cup unsweetened cocoa powder
- 1 teaspoon baking soda
- ½ teaspoon salt
- 1⅓ cups cold water
- ¾ cup canola oil
- 2 teaspoons vanilla extract
- 1 cup vegan chocolate chips (optional)

FROSTING

- ½ cup Earth Balance, vegan butter, or vegan shortening, at room temperature
- 1 teaspoon vanilla extract
- ¾ cup unsweetened cocoa powder
- 3 cups powdered sugar
- 3 tablespoons soy milk

CAKE

Preheat the oven to 350°F.

Grease and flour two 9-inch round cake pans.

Sift the flour, sugar, cocoa powder, baking soda, and salt into a medium bowl.

In a large bowl, mix the water, oil, and vanilla.

Fold the dry ingredients into the liquid ingredients, and mix until just combined.

Divide the batter into the two pans, and sprinkle half the chocolate chips onto each pan.

Bake for 25 minutes, or until a toothpick inserted into the center comes out clean.

Cool the cakes in the pans on wire racks for at least 15 minutes.

Slide a spatula or knife around the edge of each pan to loosen the cakes, and gently flip them out onto plates. Allow them to cool completely.

FROSTING

Beat the Earth Balance or shortening in a large bowl or stand mixer until fluffy.

Add the vanilla, and gradually beat in the cocoa powder.

Gradually beat in the powdered sugar, beating until well blended, and thin the frosting until a nice spreadable consistency is reached by gradually adding the soy milk a teaspoon or so at a time.

ASSEMBLY

Place one cake, chocolate chip–side up, on a plate, and spread the frosting on the top.

Set the second cake on top of the first, and frost the top and sides.

The cake can be made a day ahead of when you plan to eat it.

FRAGILITY

If you're used to making cakes with animal products, this cake will seem more fragile, requiring a gentler touch to get it out of the pan. Make sure it cools sufficiently before releasing it.

Pineapple Upside-Down Cake

A twentieth-century American classic, this recipe works best with a springform pan. It's possible to substitute regular pineapple chunks for the machine-cut rings, and you could leave out the maraschino cherries, but aesthetically the rings and cherries are what make this cake so visually appealing.

- ½ cup Earth Balance, vegan butter, or vegan shortening
- ½ cup brown sugar
- 1 can pineapple slices
- maraschino cherries
- 2½ cups all-purpose flour
- 1⅓ cups granulated sugar
- 2 teaspoons baking powder
- ½ teaspoon salt
- ½ cup canola oil
- ¾ cup soy milk
- ¼ cup juice from the canned pineapple
- 1 teaspoon vanilla extract
- ½ cup unsweetened applesauce

Preheat the oven to 350°F.

In a small saucepan, melt the Earth Balance and add the brown sugar.

Stir over low heat until the sugar dissolves, and remove from the heat.

Grease and flour a 10-inch springform pan, and wrap aluminum foil around the bottom, folded up on the sides an inch or so, to catch the drips.

Pour the Earth Balance and brown sugar mixture into the pan, spreading it evenly across the bottom.

Arrange the pineapple rings on top of the Earth Balance and sugar mixture, 1 ring in the center and 6 rings around the sides, and place a maraschino cherry in the middle of each ring.

In a large bowl, combine the flour, sugar, baking powder, and salt.

Add the canola oil, soy milk, pineapple juice, vanilla, and applesauce. Stir until everything is well combined.

Pour the batter over the pineapple slices, and bake for 50 minutes, or until a toothpick inserted into the center comes out clean.

Run a spatula or knife around the edge of the pan to loosen the cake.

When it has cooled, remove the pan's outer ring. Gently invert the cake onto a serving plate, and remove the bottom panel of the springform pan.

TIMING

Allow the cake to cool, but don't leave it in its pan for an extended period. If the sugar at the bottom gets too cool, it will stick to the sides of the pan when you try to plate it.

Apple Pie

Almost all the apples you'll find in the supermarket today are what our ancestors would have called "baking apples," which mean they'll work fine in a pie. "Eating apples"—varieties that are soft, pleasant to bite into, have an appealing mouth-feel, and are delicious without being cooked—are much rarer, available only seasonally or not at all because they don't do well sitting in warehouses for months or in trucks being transported thousands of miles. One of the few eating apples you'll see in the supermarket today is the Macintosh. This means you can use whatever apples are cheap in your apple pie, because they're all meant for baking. A lot of people like Granny Smiths for pies, but they aren't very sweet. Honeycrisps do better with the sweetness, and Braeburns have spicy elements in addition to their sweetness and tartness.

PASTRY CRUST
1 cup vegan shortening
2¼ cups flour
¾ teaspoon salt
½ cup ice water

Preheat the oven to 425°F.

PASTRY

In the bowl of a mixer or a large bowl, beat the shortening until smooth.

Stir in the flour and salt, mixing until the pastry is ragged.

Pour in the water and stir until a loose dough forms.

Separate the pastry into two balls.

On a floured surface, flatten the dough with a rolling pin. Cover the dough with plastic wrap to make it easier to roll, or add more flour if the dough sticks. Roll the dough thin enough to completely cover a 9-inch pie plate.

FILLING

7 cups thin apple slices (from 6 or 8 peeled and cored apples)

2 tablespoons lemon juice

½ cup granulated sugar

3 tablespoons flour

½ teaspoon ground cinnamon

Press the sheet of dough into a 9-inch pie plate, leaving the extra dough hanging over the sides.

FILLING

In a large bowl, toss the apple slices with the lemon juice.

In a small bowl, mix together the sugar, flour, and cinnamon, and sprinkle over the apple slices, tossing until well coated.

Put the apple mixture in the pie shell.

ASSEMBLY

Roll out the second ball of pastry to more than 9 inches.

Cover the pie with the second sheet of pastry. Press the top pastry to the bottom pastry along the rim, creating a seal. Trim the remaining overhanging pastry by running a knife around the edge.

Cut steam vent holes in the center with a knife.

Bake at 425°F for 15 minutes, then reduce the oven temperature to 350°F and bake for 40 minutes longer, or until the crust is golden.

Let cool before cutting into the pie.

PERFECT PASTRY

The pursuit of perfectly flaky pastry consumes years of the lives of some bakers, and the quality of the results is subjective. Some people love pastry that's slightly gooey, or slightly crisp, while others will turn up their noses. One truism is that it gets easier the more often you do it. Other tricks include refrigerating the pastry dough for an hour before rolling it out, but this recipe works well as long as the water you use is very cold.

Kitchen Staples

Salsa Fresca

Also called pico de gallo, *salsa fresca is a delicious fresh salsa to go with Mexican food. Roll it into your burrito, pour it on tacos, or just eat it with corn chips. In this recipe, don't skimp on the salt—it has been demonized in the health care industry, but you'll be eating small quantities of it in this recipe anyway.*

- 4 very ripe tomatoes, diced, or 1 can diced tomatoes
- 1 small onion, finely chopped
- 2 tablespoons chopped fresh cilantro
- 1 serrano pepper or 1 jalapeño pepper, seeded and minced
- juice of 1 lime
- 1 garlic clove, crushed and minced
- ¼ teaspoon ground cumin
- salt

Combine all the ingredients in a bowl.

Refrigerate for an hour or longer before serving.

⚘ FRESH TOMATOES

See the notes at the bottom of page 48 and on page 93 for some ideas about the value of fresh versus canned tomatoes.

⚘ THE SLATER IBÁÑEZ BOOKS

Slater Ibáñez hires Mason once in a while when he needs a mooky Anglo to work as his front man. Slater doesn't cook—a house guest pointed out that his stove didn't work, which was news to him—so out of necessity he's a connoisseur of the vegan options in Los Angeles's multitudinous low-end eateries. With so much Latin American cuisine in the metropolis, salsa fresca is something of an art form.

From Slater's creator: "Slater Ibáñez is only interested in two kinds of guys: the ones he wants to punch, and the ones he sleeps with. Things get interesting when they start to overlap." Check out Slater's adventures at slater.dagmarmiura.com.

Chimichurri

Used in Latin American cooking as a grilling sauce for meat, chimichurri also works great to slather on vegetables before you barbecue them, or on tofu, tempeh, or jackfruit.

- 4 garlic cloves, crushed
- ½ bunch fresh parsley
- 3 stems cilantro (optional)
- 1 hot chili pepper, such as jalapeño or habanero, cut in half and seeded
- ¼ cup olive oil
- 1 teaspoon fresh oregano, or ½ teaspoon dried oregano
- 1 teaspoon vinegar
- juice of ½ lime
- ½ teaspoon red pepper flakes
- salt

Combine all the ingredients in a food processor and pulse until well combined.

If you don't have a food processor, mince the garlic, chop the parsley, cilantro, and peppers, and whisk all the ingredients together in a bowl.

Tomato Sauce

Supermarket tomatoes aren't good anymore (see the note on page 93), so it's not necessary to make this sauce with fresh tomatoes, unless you find them cheap and ripe, or grow them yourself and have too many lying around. This sauce works great on vegetables or pasta. For a thicker sauce, to use as an ingredient in a meatloaf, for example, use more tomato paste and cook it a little longer.

- 2 tablespoons olive oil
- ½ cup chopped onion
- 3 garlic cloves, minced
- 2 cans diced tomatoes, or 5 large ripe tomatoes, diced
- ¼ cup tomato paste
- 1 tablespoon dried basil, or 2 tablespoons chopped fresh basil
- salt

Heat the olive oil in a saucepan over medium heat and add the onion and garlic, stirring and cooking until translucent.

Add the tomatoes and their liquid, and add the tomato paste.

Bring to a boil and reduce the heat to a simmer, cooking for about 10 minutes.

Stir in the basil and salt and simmer, uncovered, for another 10 minutes.

Spicy Slather Sauce

Perfect to garnish veggie burgers or to dip crudités or veggie nuggets into, this sauce has a tasty amalgam of flavors that go with almost anything.

- ⅔ cup mayonnaise (see the note on page 83)
- 1 teaspoon tamari
- 2 tablespoons sambal oelek
- ½ teaspoon agave syrup

In a bowl, combine all the ingredients and mix well with a spatula.

Cashew Cheese Sauce

This quick recipe is light and creamy and goes well over steamed vegetables, similar to a traditional white sauce, or over noodles, like a carbonara. Use unflavored, unsweetened soy milk or nut milk instead of water to make the sauce even creamier. Once cooked, the sauce will keep for at least four days in the refrigerator.

Four other cheese sauces appear in this book: one that also uses cashews with a longer list of ingredients (page 67), one that uses nutritional yeast but no cashews (page 65), nacho cheese sauce (page 120), and a deleicious ricotta (page 76).

2½ cups water

1 cup raw cashews

¼ cup nutritional yeast

2 teaspoons lemon juice

1 teaspoon salt

If you don't have a high-speed blender, cover the cashews in ½ inch of water and soak for at least two hours, then drain. (If they aren't soaked, a standard blender will produce a grainy sauce.)

Blend all the ingredients in a blender until smooth and creamy.

In a saucepan over medium-high heat, cook the sauce, whisking constantly until it thickens, about 4 minutes.

❋ REJUVELAC

The defining characteristic of cheese isn't animal fat but rather fermentation. A popular vegan fermented cheese base is Ann Wigmore's rejuvelac liquid. It's made with grain and sits on the counter for eight days as it ferments, so preparing rejuvelac is beyond the scope of this book, but look it up if you want to delve into vegan cheese-making—rejuvelac makes incredibly flavorful cheeses.

Nacho Cheese Sauce

Like cashew cheese sauce (page 119), nacho cheese sauce goes great over steamed vegetables or in Mexican dishes like quesadillas (page 33). Using chipotle gives it a smoky taste, but be wary when shopping for ground chipotle—several of the commercial "chipotle" products on the market contain a mere dusting of chipotle or other peppers mixed with flavoring chemicals and a whole lot of salt. But if you look hard, it is possible to find unadulterated ground chipotles.

- ¼ cup flour
- 1½ cups soy milk or nut milk (see the note below)
- ½ cup nutritional yeast
- ¼ cup olive oil
- 2 tablespoons tahini
- 1 teaspoon salt
- ½ teaspoon garlic powder
- ½ teaspoon paprika
- ½ teaspoon ground chipotle pepper or ground cayenne pepper

Place the flour in a saucepan. Pour in the soy milk or nut milk and whisk until combined.

Mix in the remaining ingredients.

Over medium-high heat, whisk constantly until the sauce thickens.

⇒ UNFLAVORED MILK

Nothing ruins a mouthful of cheesiness like a blast of vanilla. Even professional chefs sometimes make the mistake of using vanilla-flavored soy milk or nut milk in savory sauces. Vanilla tastes great in your morning coffee or over your muesli, but it will ruin a cheese sauce. Make sure your milk is unflavored and unsweetened, and if you don't have the plain version on hand, just use water instead.

⇒ THICKNESS

A thinner sauce is nice to drizzle on vegetables, but to get a thicker version, cook it longer, whisking constantly, and let it cool for a few minutes.

Aioli

In Europe, aioli comes in a wide variety of forms, sometimes with eggs and dairy and Darwin knows what else mixed in. The common elements, however, are always garlic and olive oil. This makes an excellent sandwich spread, like mayonnaise, or a dip for artichokes (see below). It's not traditional, but in Billy Blood, *Ned adds a little habanero to give it a kick.*

- ½ cup of raw cashews
- 2 garlic cloves
- 2 tablespoons lemon juice
- ½ teaspoon mustard powder
- ½ teaspoon salt
- ½ teaspoon ground habanero pepper (optional)
- 3 tablespoons olive oil

If you don't have a high-speed blender, soak the cashews in water for at least 2 hours, then drain. (If they aren't soaked, the aioli will be grainy in a regular blender.)

Put the cashews, garlic, lemon juice, mustard, and salt into the blender and blend until smooth.

With the blender running at medium speed, slowly pour the olive oil into the mixture.

Finish with a blast at high speed.

ARTICHOKES

This aioli make a perfect dip for steamed artichoke. Artichokes are easy to cook: wash them thoroughly, making sure no dirt remains deep between the leaves. Snip off the tips of the leaves with scissors, then steam them for 30 minutes. After they're cooked, pull off a leaf, dip the inside end in the aioli, and pull it between your teeth. When all the leaves are gone, use a spoon to scrape away the prickly inedible choke, and enjoy the soft, delicious heart below it.

Acknowledgments

I've tried to cite my inspirations in the introduction to some of the recipes in this book, but I also have to thank all the creative and motivated vegan cooks who have come up with fun and innovative ways to combine and prepare the wide variety of edible plants that nature provides for us. Don't be afraid to experiment, and share your creations with the rest of us vegans online!

About the Author

Henrietta Flores, author of the Quick Vegan Travel Guides series, has taught English as a second language to adults in the United States and abroad. She is an avid traveler and has learned over the years how to eat vegan on five continents, picking up some cooking chops along the way. Having committed to veganism in the 1990s, she believes in compassion for all creatures. Henrietta lives in California with a spoiled dog, a pair of cats, and a serious Scrabble addiction.

About the Photographer

Cory Mac a'Ghobhainn is an animal rights activist, ESL teacher, and artist. She lives in Los Angeles and likes to organize protests and take pics of food and cats.

Index

A

active yeast 88
agave 50, 52, **53**, 54, 59, 75, 89, 118
Aioli 121
almond milk. *See* nut milk
almonds 15, 26, 50, 58, 83
animal welfare **3**
apple cider vinegar 52, 53, 97
apple corer 27
Apple Pie **110**
apples 27, **110**
applesauce 100, 105, 108
apricots 26
aquafaba 34, **96**
artichokes 60, **121**
Asian Ginger Dressing **54**
asparagus 77
Atomic Pinto Beans 92
avocados **32**, **101**

B

Baked Doughnuts 97
Baked Eggplant 64
balsamic vinegar 42
banana 23
basil 36, 42, 48, 55, 58, 76, 117
beans **68**
bell peppers 29, 40, 42, 47, 62, 69, 70, 78, 83
besan. *See* garbanzo flour
Billy Blood 34, 68, 121
black salt **29**
blueberries 26, 27
Bob's Red Mill 26

bok choy 69
bread 23, 42, 49, **88**
broccoli 69
broth. *See* stock
brown sugar 22, 78, 98, 100, 105, 108
bulgur 37, 88
butternut squash 73

C

Caesar Salad *50*
cane sugar 53
canned tomatoes **93**
canola oil 24, 67, 100, 102, 105, 106, 108
caprese salad 48
carrots 36, 43, 80, 89
Cashew Cheese Sauce 33
cashews 15, 55, 67, 76, 119, 121
cauliflower *86*
cayenne pepper 32, 42, 59, 70, 92, 120
celery 36, 42, 43, 68, 83
celiac disease 9, 13
cheese, cream 104
cheese, ricotta 76
cheese sauce 65, 67, 119, 120
chemistry of vegan cooking 24
chickpeas. *See* garbanzos
chili oil 75
chili peppers 69, 116
chili powder 68, 70, 92
Chimichurri 116
Chinese noodles 75
chipotle pepper 70, **120**
chocolate cake 106
chocolate chips 98, 106
Chocolate Layer Cake 106
chocolate mousse 101

cilantro 32, 69, 114, 116
cinnamon 23, 97, 105, 111
cocoa powder 101, 102, 106
coconut milk 69
coconut oil 100, 101
coffee 20
Cold Chinese Noodles with Sesame Sauce *75*
Cold Soba Noodles with Dipping Sauce *72*
coriander 68, 69
Cory 60, 90, 125
cracked wheat 37, 88
cranberries 26
cream cheese 104
cream of tartar 96
Creamy Italian Dressing **55**
croutons 49, 50
Croutons **49**
Crusty Bread 88
cucumbers 42, 47
cucumber salad 47
cumin 64, 68, 69, 83, 92, 114
Curry 69

D

dairy products **5**
dates 26
The Desert Rats 29, 33, 67
dill 73, 83
doughnuts 97
dressing 50, 52, 53, 54, 55

E

Earth Balance 22, 24, 65, 97, 98, 104, 106, 108
eggplant 64
environmentalism **4**
Espresso *20*
estrogen 11

BOLDFACE PAGE NUMBERS = EXPLANATORY TEXT • *ITALICS* = PHOTOGRAPH

F

factory farming 48
fat 7
fettucine 77
figs 60
fingerling potatoes 69
flaxseed 105
flour 24, 36, 62, 65, 80, 88, 90, 97, 98, 100, 102, 105, 106, 108, 110, 111, 120
flour tortillas 33
French Toast 23
Fried Tempeh with Plum Sauce *78*
fruit 27
Fruit Smoothie 27

G

garbanzo flour 60
garbanzos 34, **60**, 96
garlic 34, 36, 42, 50, 52, 53, 54, 55, 58, 59, 60, 64, 68, 69, 75, 76, 77, 78, 83, 92, 114, 116, 117, 121
garlic powder 65, 67, 120
Gazpacho **42**
Gilbert 33
ginger 54, 59, 69, 72, 75, 78
glass noodles 75
gluten **8**, 13
goddess dressing 52
granulated sugar 47, 50, 62, 75, 89, 96, 97, 101, 102, 111
grapes 27
green cauliflower *86*
green goddess dressing 52
green onions 37, 64, 72, 75, 83
green peas 89
Guacamole **32**

H

habanero pepper 69, 116, 121
heirloom tomatoes 48
high-performance blender. *See* high-speed blender
high-speed blender 11, **14**, 27, 40, 53, 54, 55, 60, 67, 76, 90, 101, 119, 121
hot dogs 70
hot dog topping 70
Hummus *34*
hydrogenated oils 7

I

immersion blender 43
The Invisible Arrow 76, 89, 92
Italian dressing 55

J

jackfruit 116
jalapeño pepper 47, 68, 69, 114, 116
Just Mayo 83

K

kidney beans 68
kiwi 27
kosher salt 48

L

lasagna 64
lemon juice 26, 34, 36, 37, 42, 55, 59, 67, 77, 83, 89, 111, 119, 121
lemon zest 81
lentils 43
lime juice 32, 47, 68, 114, 116

M

Mac and Cheese *67*
macaroni 67
mandoline **47**
The Man from Grapalia 78
maple syrup 23, 24, 52, 73, 81
maraschino cherries 108
margarine 7
marinara **63**
marinara sauce 62, 76
marjoram 90
Mason 1, 34, 48, 68, 69, 76, 89, 92, 114
mayonnaise **83**, 118
meringue 96
Meringue Cookies 96
mint 37
mirepoix **43**
mirin 59, **72**
miso 50
Muesli **26**
mushroom gravy 80, 90
Mushroom Gravy *90*
mushrooms 60, 69, 70, 77, 90
mustard 81
mustard powder 36, 50, 81, 121

N

nacho cheese sauce 33, 120
Nacho Cheese Sauce 120
navy beans 68
Ned 2, 29, 33, 43, 48, 52, 67, 68, 76, 78, 121
1950s Peas and Carrots 89
nutmeg 23, 97, 105
nut milk 22, 26, 97, 98, 102, 104
nutritional yeast **13**, 23, 29, 36, 50, 58, 65, 67, 76, 90, 119, 120
nuts **15**, **58**

oatmeal **22**, 100
Oatmeal 22
Oatmeal Cookies 100
oats 22, 26
old-fashioned oats 100
olive oil 24, 37, 42, 48, **49**, 50, 52, 53, 54, 55, 59, 62, 64, 65, 67, 70, 77, 78, 86, 90, 116, 120, 121
olives 60
Onion, Pepper, and Mushroom Hash 70
onion powder 55, 67, 78
onions 29, 32, 36, 42, 43, 47, 59, 60, 62, 68, 69, 70, 77, 80, 83, 90, 92, 114, 117
oranges 27, 60
oregano 49, 55, 68, 116

paleo diet **9**
Pancakes *24*
panko 67
paprika 64, **65**, 77, 81, 120
parsley 29, 34, 37, 42, 49, 52, 55, 76, 77, 83, 116
Parsnip Pearl Barley Soup 43
parsnips 43
pasta 58, 76, 77
pastry **111**
pâté 36
peaches 60
peanut butter **98**
Peanut Butter Cookies *98*
peanut oil 75
pearl barley 43
pecans 26, 98
Peggy 1, 2, 34, 42, 50, 68, 69, 70, 83
pesto **58**, 60
Pesto on Zucchini Noodles 58

phyllo **81**
pico de gallo 114
pineapple 27, 108
Pineapple Upside-Down Cake *108*
pinto beans 92
pizza crust 62, **63**
plum jam 78
plums 78
plum sauce 78
poblano peppers 68
potatoes 36
powdered sugar 97, 104, 106
protein **5**
puff pastry **80**

Quesadillas 33

raisins 26, 105
raspberries 27
Rationalist Dressing 52
Raw Tomato and Red Pepper Soup *40*
Reach for the Sky 68, 69
red food coloring 102
red pepper flakes 54, 78, 92, 116
Red Velvet Cake **102**
red wine 80, 81
red wine vinegar 42
rejuvelac **119**
relish 83
rice **69**
rice wine vinegar 47, 54, 75
ricotta **76**
Roasted Green Cauliflower Steaks 86
Roasted Squash 73
romaine 50
Rubber Band Ball 42, 43, 50, 70

sage 36, 73, 90
salad 45, 47, 48, 50
Salsa Fresca *114*
sambal oelek 54, **59**, 118
San-J 14
sausages 70
Secret Avocado Chocolate Mousse 101
seitan **13**, 77, 81
Seitan Stroganoff **77**
Seitan Wellington and Mushroom Gravy 80
serrano pepper 114
sesame oil 47, 54, 59, 75
sesame sauce 75
sesame seeds 47, 59, 72
shallots 60
shortening 104, 110
Signs Point to Yes 48
Slater Ibáñez 114
smoked paprika 64, 65, 81
smoothie 27
soba noodles 72
Socca **60**
soup 39, 42, 43
soy **11**
soy milk 22, 23, 24, 26, 65, 67, 97, 98, 102, 104, 106, 108, 120
soy sauce 14, **52**
spaghetti noodles 75
spicy brown mustard 53
Spicy Cucumber Salad *47*
Spicy Slather Sauce 118
spinach 29, 76, 80
split peas 43
springform pan 108
squash 73
sriracha **59**
stock 65, 68, 76, 77, 90
strawberries 27
stroganoff 77

BOLDFACE PAGE NUMBERS = EXPLANATORY TEXT • *ITALICS* = PHOTOGRAPH

sugar **9**. *See also* granulated sugar; *See also* powdered sugar
sun-dried tomatoes 60, 64
sunflower seeds 26, 36, 83
superfoods 8
Sweet Mustard Dressing **53**

Tabbouleh **37**
tahini **14**, 52, 75, 77, 120
tamari **14**, **52**, 54, 59, 70, 72, 75, 78, 83, 90, 118
tarragon 77
tempeh **11**, 64, 78, 83, 116
Tempeh Salad *83*
teriyaki sauce 59
Teriyaki Tofu 59
Thin-Crust Pizza with Sliced Red Peppers 62
thyme 36, 73, 81, 90
tofu **11**, 29, 48, 50, 59, 69, 76, 116
Tofu Caprese Salad 48
Tofu Scramble **29**
tomatoes 32, **37**, 40, 42, **48**, 64, 68, 69, 92, **93**, 114, 117
tomato paste 64, 117
Tomato Sauce 117
tomato soup 40
tortillas 33
triglycerides 9
turmeric 29, 65, 69

unflavored milk **120**

vanilla 120
vanilla extract 97, 98, 102, 104, 105, 106, 108
vegan dogs 70
Vegan Ricotta and Spinach-Stuffed Shells 76
vegan sausages 70
vegetable broth. *See* stock
vegetable stock. *See* stock
Veggie Pâté **36**
vinegar 78, 102, 116
vital wheat gluten 13

walnuts 26
White Bean Chili 68

yeast, active 62

Z

zucchini 58, 64, 105
Zucchini Bread 105
zucchini noodles 58

www.ingramcontent.com/pod-product-compliance
Lightning Source LLC
Chambersburg PA
CBHW051247110526
44588CB00025B/2906